E-LEARNING FUNDAMENTALS

A Practical Guide

Diane Elkins and Desirée Pinder

PRESS

ATD Press is an internationally renowned source of insightful and practical information on talent development, workplace learning, and professional development.

ATD Press
1640 King Street
Alexandria, VA 22314 USA

Ordering information: Books published by ATD Press can be purchased by visiting ATD's website at www.td.org/books or by calling 800.628.2783 or 703.683.8100.

Library of Congress Control Number: 2015936412

ISBN-10: 1-56286-947-7
ISBN-13: 978-1-56286-947-2
e-ISBN: 978-1-60728-272-3

ATD Press Editorial Staff
Director: Kristine Luecker
Manager: Christian Green
Community of Practice Manager, Learning Technologies: Justin Brusino
Developmental Editor: Kathryn Stafford
Cover Design: Julia Prymak, Pryme Design
Text Design: Maggie Hyde
Printed by Versa Press, Inc., East Peoria, IL, www.versapress.com

CONTENTS

PREFACE

I still remember my first e-learning conference. It was October 2000, and I had recently been tapped to be in charge of e-learning production for the company I was working for at the time. I knew Excel, which made me the "techie" on the team. Now that I was responsible for converting hours and hours of instructor -led courses to e-learning, I tried to get my hands on whatever I could to find out what I needed to know. Back then, it wasn't as easy as today. I didn't know what I didn't know. At the conference, my boss and I attended sessions on one subject that raised questions about 10 other subjects. And many of the speakers were throwing out terms we didn't know. While we left with more questions than answers, we figured it out. We created some courses that were very successful, but it wasn't always a smooth process.

Fast forward several years. I joined forces with Desirée Pinder to start our own e-learning development company, what is now Artisan E-Learning. By this time, a whole industry had been built up around e-learning. But, today, for folks just getting started, it can still be challenging to jump in. As opposed to 15 years ago, you now have access to all sorts of information about e-learning strategy and development—but perhaps too much information. It can still be hard to know where to get started, to know which sessions to attend at a conference, to know which blogs to read, and sometimes just to know what any of them are talking about!

That's where this book comes in. Desirée and I started teaching a class at the University of North Florida to help people who wanted to get up and running with e-learning. The early version of this book was written to serve as the text for that course. For those students, we wanted to provide a comprehensive overview of the e-learning process, from the ground up; we want to do the same for you today.

We hope that this book helps point you in the right direction and gives you a boost of knowledge and confidence as you start your e-learning journey.

Bon voyage!

Diane Elkins

INTRODUCTION

E-Learning Fundamentals: A Practical Guide offers a comprehensive overview of the e-learning process, from the ground up. While other books and resources may go deep into one aspect or another (gamification, instructional design, mobile), this book offers a little bit of everything—a base of knowledge that will help you understand what goes into e-learning development.

Book chapters are organized according to the ADDIE model (analyze, design, develop, implement, evaluate), which is widely used to manage training development.

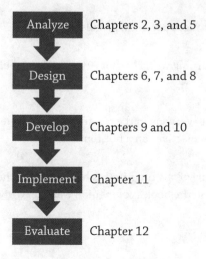

Analyze	Chapters 2, 3, and 5
Design	Chapters 6, 7, and 8
Develop	Chapters 9 and 10
Implement	Chapter 11
Evaluate	Chapter 12

First, chapter 1 defines e-learning and examines the advantages and disadvantages that different types of e-learning offer. It introduces terms and jargon every user should know. Chapter 2 describes how to develop a strategy, from an organizational and managerial perspective. Chapter 3 examines how to put a plan in place. Chapter 4 then provides an overview of the various technology decisions you'll need to make.

The second half of the book looks at self-paced e-learning development from a tactical perspective, continuing to follow the steps in the ADDIE model. Chapter 5 covers the analysis phase, where you'll examine the business, audience, and technology needs for your courses. Chapters 6, 7, and 8 examine design considerations, such as testing and interactivity, as well as how to develop a design document. Chapters 9 and 10 describe the development phase, how to write a course with the use of storyboards, and how to develop a prototype to start a course off right. Chapter 11 covers implementation, how to prepare your audience for the course, with detailed tips for success. Chapter 12 discusses the different levels of evaluation you can use to see if your course met its objectives. Finally, chapter 13 offers a glimpse of ways to prepare for the future. Along the way, you'll get practical advice, checklists, templates, resource tips, and process details for everything from identifying organizational needs to writing storyboards to ensuring the quality of your online courses.

Be sure to watch for these helpful features:

 Tips From the Pros: Get expert advice on how to put the concepts in this book into action.

 Been There; Done That: Benefit from someone else's experience so you don't have to learn these lessons the hard way.

 Dive Deeper: Here you'll find references to books and other resources to help you learn more about a certain subject.

 Caution: Watch out for these potential pitfalls.

 Jargon Alert: The e-learning world has lots of special vocabulary and abbreviations. Learn the important ones here.

 The Great Debate: Not everyone in the e-learning world agrees on everything. Here you can learn about different perspectives on a hot topic.

 For Your Toolbox: Many of the tools in this book (such as checklists and forms) are available for download on the book's companion website: www.td.org/elearningtools.

1

WHAT IS E-LEARNING?

Have you ever learned how to do something from a YouTube video? Ever found an answer to a question from Wikipedia or a discussion forum? Any time you learn something from an electronic source, that is e-learning—electronic learning.

In a more formal sense (and for the purposes of this book), e-learning is any course or structured learning event that uses an electronic medium to meet its objectives. It can have many of the same elements of more traditional learning (text, audio, tests, homework), but a computer is used to meet or enhance the learning objectives.

The pages and chapters that follow provide what you need to know to decide if a given learning need will be suitable for e-learning and if so, how to take that concept to a fully executed self-paced e-learning course.

Types of E-Learning

E-learning can be divided into three main types. These types are based on the use of an instructor, timing of the course, and involvement with others. Selecting the appropriate type involves considering the learner's prior knowledge, learning speed, time available, and geographic separation. These are the three main types of e-learning: synchronous learning, asynchronous learning, and cohort learning.

The main focus of this book is asynchronous learning; however, synchronous and cohort techniques are defined here for purposes of comparison.

Synchronous Learning

Synchronous learning occurs when an instructor and learners are together at the same time—but not necessarily in the same physical place.

Traditional classroom learning is a great example of synchronous learning. During a traditional classroom session, learners meet at a set time, have discussions, and are tested together.

A synchronous e-learning course uses the same concept. At a set period of time, an instructor and one or more learners participate in an electronic learning event using a platform such as Adobe Connect or GoToMeeting. This format can be called a webcast, webinar, or virtual classroom.

This type of training may include the instructor speaking, visuals such as PowerPoint slides or desktop sharing, discussion via chat (as shown in Figure 1-1), poll questions, and even activities via breakout rooms.

FIGURE 1-1: EXAMPLE OF A SYNCHRONOUS E-LEARNING COURSE

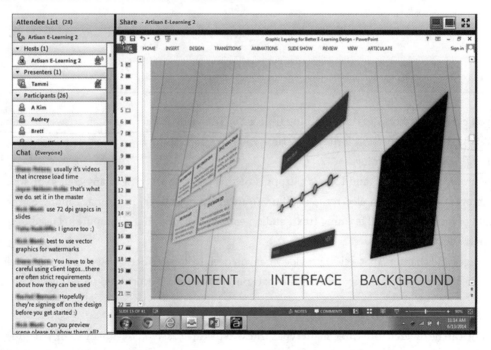

Asynchronous Learning

Asynchronous learning, or self-paced learning, is the opposite of synchronous learning. It occurs when the instructor and learners do not participate at the same time. Often there is no instructor at all, as in the self-paced branching scenario in Figure 1-2.

FIGURE 1-2: EXAMPLE OF AN ASYNCHRONOUS LEARNING COURSE

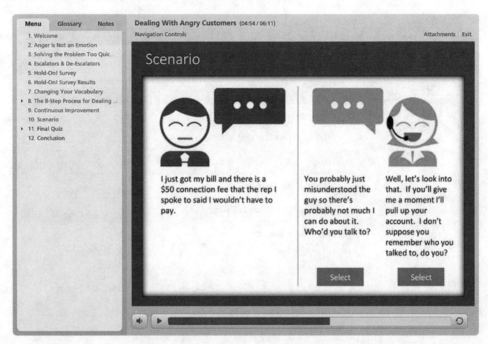

In the world of traditional education, think of homework as asynchronous learning. If learners are given an activity to complete on their own time by themselves, the learning is asynchronous.

In the world of e-learning, a self-paced course that can be accessed at any time and does not require the involvement of an instructor or peers is considered asynchronous.

Cohort Learning

Cohort learning has an instructor, and learners complete activities such as readings, videos, discussions, assignments, and projects. There is a specified beginning and end date, but within the course timeframes, participants learn and communicate on their own time.

For example, in a synchronous leadership webinar, all participants log on to their computers at 2 p.m. on Tuesday and participate in the presentation until it is over at 4 p.m. With the cohort model, the learners typically log on at the beginning of the week and could then read the materials, complete the activities, and discuss issues with other classmates at any time during the week.

FIGURE 1-3: EXAMPLE OF THE COHORT MODEL

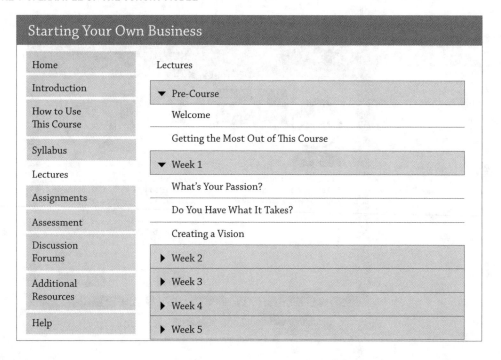

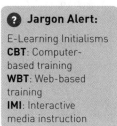

Jargon Alert:

E-Learning Initialisms
CBT: Computer-
based training
WBT: Web-based
training
IMI: Interactive
media instruction

Cohort learning includes an instructor who gives and grades tests and other assign-ments. This model is popular in higher education using platforms such as Blackboard.

In addition to traditional for-credit courses, some universities are now offering this type of course free and open to the public, using platforms such as Coursera. Often called MOOCs (massive open online course), some of these free and open programs can have 10,000 or even 100,000 learners.

Blended Learning

Blended learning uses two or more learning events in different formats. For example, you may develop asynchronous e-learning modules to present factual information, and then invite learners to participate in classroom instruction where they can have face-to-face discussions or hands-on practice.

Advantages and Disadvantages of Asynchronous E-Learning

There is rarely a decision that has to be made in life that doesn't have advantages and disadvantages for both sides. The same is true for what learning format you choose for your course. It is important to weigh the advantages and disadvantages of the possibilities before you make a final decision.

Which is better: traditional classroom learning or e-learning? Or, is a blended solution best? Take a look at the advantages and disadvantages of e-learning so you can decide what is best for your situation.

Advantages of Asynchronous E-Learning

Asynchronous e-learning offers a number of unique advantages:

Viewed Anywhere

E-learning programs can be viewed anywhere in the world where a computer is available. You can choose to present your course in these formats:

- **Computer**—The course could be permanently placed on your computer's hard drive. Though this takes up hard drive space, it could be more convenient than carrying a disk or having to connect to a network.

- **Internet**—Your course could be housed on the Internet. This convenient method allows for quick changes to the course, does not take up valuable space on your hard drive, and does not require that your computer have a CD drive to be able to view it.

- **Intranet**—Your course could be placed on an internal company network that can only be accessed by employees of the company. This increases security, but sometimes makes it more difficult for remote employees to access the courses.

- **Mobile device**—Your course could be viewed on a mobile device such as a phone or tablet. The course could be downloaded to the device, viewed in an Internet browser, or packaged as an app.

- **Disk**—Generally, a course will fit on a CD-ROM, DVD, or USB drive. The advantages to having your course on a disk are that it is portable and the computer does not need an Internet connection. If you plan to use this method, be sure to consider your student's hardware now and in the near future. Fewer and fewer computers are even being sold with CD and DVD drives.

Used Anytime

Because of time-zone differences and people's busy schedules, it is valuable to have a solution that allows participants to learn when they can fit it into their schedules. If they want to view an online course during lunch, during a regular workday, or at 3 a.m., they can.

Less Expensive for Many Users

E-learning is an expensive solution if only a few people are learning from it; however, if many people take the course, it could cost significantly less than the traditional classroom model. For example, if a trainer is required in locations throughout the world, you could save on travel and lodging costs with an e-learning program.

Tracking Capabilities

An e-learning course can be set up to track such things as who took a course, how long a person spent reviewing the course materials, and the test scores. This can be very valuable information, especially for mandatory or certification classes that require proof of completion.

Self-Paced Learning

Learning speed can vary greatly from person to person. E-learning courses allow studying at one's own pace. Slower learners can feel free to take their time learning information, and faster learners can go through the materials at a quicker pace and still get the information they need from the course.

Review Tool

Once material has been learned, it is possible for learners to go back and review areas that they don't remember or for which they need some pointers. This is helpful for seldom-used or complex concepts or procedures.

Performance Support for Just-in-Time Learning

Sometimes employees do not need a full course. They just need a little bit of information to help them with what they are doing at the moment. E-learning can help meet the immediate need for training. Examples of just-in-time training include a help menu in a computer program or an online checklist to prepare for a meeting, as shown in Figure 1-4.

FIGURE 1-4: EXAMPLE OF ONLINE PERFORMANCE SUPPORT

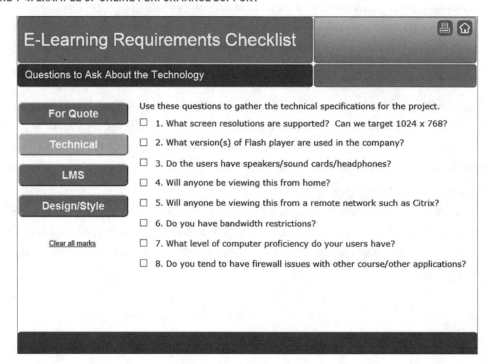

Delivered on Demand

Once a course has been developed and posted, participants can take it as soon as they need it—rather than waiting until the next time the course is offered.

Unlimited Simultaneous Users

Where classroom courses can only allow a certain number of learners per session, an e-learning course can be available to unlimited users at any given time. This can allow many people in multiple locations to get access to valuable information right away. This is useful when the entire company needs time-sensitive information and you can't wait for the trainers to get to all the locations.

Disadvantages of Asynchronous E-Learning

While e-learning can solve some of the problems of classroom learning, there can be disadvantages to using it:

Development Time and Cost

While hundreds or thousands of participants can take an e-learning course quickly, that doesn't mean it is quick to develop. Similarly, although an e-learning program may end up being cheaper per user than classroom training, it isn't cheap. Between development costs, hardware and software, and ongoing maintenance, you could spend anywhere from a few thousand to more than a million dollars. If you have a small audience or budget, e-learning may not make sense for you. Refer to chapter 3 for more information about the time and cost of e-learning.

Lack of Collaboration

Some of the best learning in a classroom often comes from the interaction with the instructor and other learners. While this collaboration is not impossible with e-learning, there will probably not be as much of it.

Technology

If the right technology is not in place, can't be afforded, or can't be supported, e-learning can be frustrating or even futile. Anyone who has tried to watch a video on a slow corporate connection knows this.

Computer Literacy

Some learners may not be computer literate. It is important to know your audience and plan, at the outset, to train learners on how to use the needed technology.

Computer Availability

Not everybody has access to a computer. If you do not supply computers to all employees in your organization, for example, it could be difficult for some to take e-learning courses.

Device Compatibility

Not all courses can be used with all types of devices, browsers, and operating systems. It is important to know what your audience has and decide if your course can be viewed by everybody in your target audience.

Unanswered Questions

In classroom instruction, it is easy for participants to get their individual questions answered. With e-learning courses, it can be difficult for participants to find answers to questions left unanswered after completing the course. The goal with developing e-learning is to answer the questions before they are asked.

Lower Energy and Excitement

Learning online does not tend to create the same kind of excitement and energy as do traditional classroom sessions, which can more easily generate learner buy-in about a particular subject. Also, a classroom session might be a refreshing break from a production line or cubicle.

Elements of an E-Learning Course

Asynchronous e-learning courses can take many shapes and sizes. However, there are certain elements that are common among most courses. Starting out with an understanding of these elements will help prepare you for discussions on planning and analysis. Each of the elements listed here is explained in more detail in the design phase discussions in chapters 6, 7, and 8. Figures 1-5 and 1-6 illustrate some of these design elements.

FIGURE 1-5: EXAMPLE OF E-LEARNING COURSE ELEMENTS

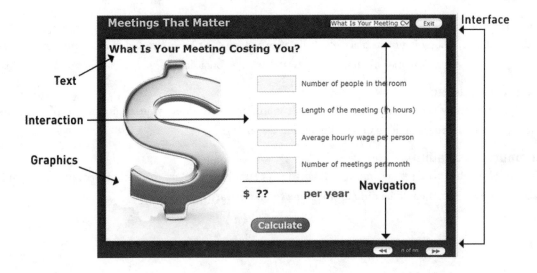

FIGURE 1-6: EXAMPLE OF E-LEARNING COURSE ELEMENTS

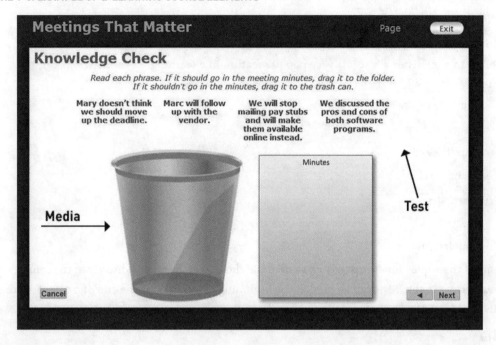

Interface

The interface is the visual framework for each screen. It includes the branding, titles, buttons, features, and navigation used throughout the course. Think of it as the elements that are the same on every screen.

Text

In an asynchronous course, text can be used either as the primary way to communicate content or as support for audio narration.

Navigation

The navigation for a course allows the learner to move through the course. Navigation buttons such as arrows, hyperlinks, and menus all guide the learner through the course. Navigation can be fixed (where the learner has to proceed in a linear fashion from the beginning to the end) or flexible (where the learner can choose where to go).

Interactions

Interactions are any events or activities that require the learner to respond in some way. Examples include a spot that the learner clicks to get additional information, a question the learner must answer, or a practice simulation. Interactions help to reinforce key teaching points and keep the learner interested and engaged. They are often the most interesting part of the e-learning course. However, they can also be the most time consuming to create.

Tests

The ability to administer a test is a very popular feature in e-learning. Tests questions can use several formats:

- multiple choice
- drag and drop
- true/false
- fill in the blank
- short answer
- essay
- simulations.

Some of these question formats (such as multiple choice) can be graded directly in the course; others (such as essay) cannot. Tests can be used at the beginning of a course, at the end of a course, at the end of individual modules, or scattered throughout the course.

Media

Technically, an e-learning course could consist of only on-screen text. But a more engaging course would use a number of different media elements, such as:

- **audio**—used to deliver the primary content, as with a narrator, or can be used in specific situations, such as an introduction from the president of a company or characters in a scenario
- **video**—can be used as the primary method of content delivery or to provide additional information for specific teaching points
- **graphics**—include still photography (stock photography or custom), clip-art pictures, illustrations, graphs, or diagrams
- **animations**—include moving graphics; for example, for a course about a manufacturing process, a moving graphic could simulate the flow through the different production departments.

Collaboration

Collaboration is the activity of learners working together to reach a learning goal. In the classroom, collaboration occurs anytime one learner turns to another and makes a comment, asks a question, or works with someone on a project. In e-learning this might occur in discussion forums or social media sites.

Discussion Forums

A discussion forum is a collaborative learning experience where questions or comments are posted and a trail of responses are posted and archived regarding the original message. Often called threaded discussions or message boards, forums are asynchronous forms of communication and message sending. Self-paced courses can encourage learners to participate in discussions about the course content. In some cases, an instructor or moderator reviews the discussions to provide guidance and answers questions.

FIGURE 1-7: ASYNCHRONOUS COURSE FEATURING AN ONLINE DISCUSSION FORUM

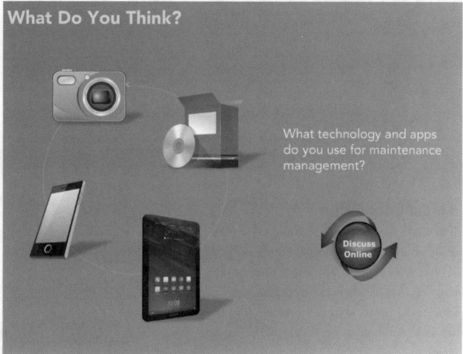

Images courtesy of Community Associations Institute.

FIGURE 1-8: ONLINE DISCUSSION FORUM LINKED FROM COURSE

> **3-1 What technology and apps do you use for maintenance management?**
> Between digital cameras, specialized software, and mobile devices such as phones and tablets, technology is helping to improve how we keep track of maintenance.
>
> What technology and apps do you use for maintenance management? Share your thoughts with other students.
>
> Posted: 7/26/2012 8:50 AM by   View Properties | Reply
> I go out to my properties and take pictures or the board sends me pictures I contact my contractors for whatever needs to be done and they are there same day with my camera I can send them a picture so they can bring the right tools to fix my problem.
>
> Posted: 5/31/2014 7:49 PM by   View Properties | Reply
> Unfortunately we are a little behind the times with this. I use Excel to track our main plumbing line maintenance. Our maintenance dept. keeps a paper log of all routine inspections, etc.
>
> ⌄ Show Quoted Messages
>
> Posted: 8/20/2012 7:19 PM by   View Properties | Reply
> we currently have a web portal where every owner can log into their account and view their workorder history and updates.
>
> Posted: 8/20/2012 8:05 PM by   View Properties | Reply
> We used to do everything on paper and finding history was a nightmare. We finally have a maintenance management system that has allowed us to integrate computer/tablets/and photos - what a difference!

Social Media Integration

Sites such as LinkedIn, Twitter, and Facebook can be used to foster collaboration. For example, a course could be given a Twitter hashtag with students encouraged to post and search for tweets using that hashtag. Some corporations have their own internal social media system (such as Yammer or Jive) that allows such communication to happen privately within the organization.

Tracking

One of the many reasons companies choose e-learning is the ability to track progress, completion, and test scores. If set up to do so, e-learning courses can send this information to be tracked. In the simplest forms, the information might be sent via an email. In more formal situations, the information is fed

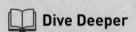 **Dive Deeper**

Social Media for Trainers: Techniques for Enhancing and Extending Learning by Jane Bozarth

The New Social Learning: Connect. Collaborate. Work., second edition by Tony Bingham and Marcia Conner

to a learning management system (LMS) that compiles and stores the information, as shown in the examples. Especially when a course is mandatory per regulation, it is important to be able to prove a learner did take and pass the course.

Summary

E-learning uses an electronic medium to allow learners to learn collaboratively or on their own, at their own pace or at the pace of a group. It has multiple advantages as well as disadvantages in comparison to other platforms. So, it's important to weigh the options and decide what is best for your particular course and objectives.

2

DEVELOPING AN E-LEARNING STRATEGY

"Everybody's doing it."

"I've heard it will save us money."

"My bonus is tied to it."

"The CEO read an article about it, and now we have to deliver 50 percent of our training online by the end of the year."

E-learning projects have been started (and have occasionally been successful) with very little thought or justification. However, most projects will benefit from thoughtful consideration of the whys and the hows before jumping right in.

This chapter helps identify the questions you need to ask and the process to follow to determine if e-learning is a good solution, the best way to approach it, and how to get everyone on board.

The Strategic Plan

There are many different models, outlines, templates, and checklists that provide guidance on how to conduct strategic planning for any issue. Some are elaborate; some are simple, but they all contain the basics: What are you trying to do? Why are you trying to do it? How are you going to get there?

While this is a simple model, it is amazing how many projects, even at a high level, get started without looking at these questions.

Benefits of a Strategic Plan

A good strategic plan can take a lot of time and effort to develop, but it can serve many purposes as well. It can help you:

- decide if you even want to embark on an e-learning journey
- generate support from key stakeholders
- request funding from internal or external sources
- reach consensus on what it will take to make the project happen
- notify everyone of potential risks and challenges
- ensure you are doing this for the right reasons
- create a common picture of what success would look like
- point you in the right direction for getting started.

In the end, any of the platitudes about proper planning (such as "if you fail to plan, you plan to fail" and "begin with the end in mind") apply to an e-learning project. The strategic plan gets you started.

Strategic Plans Versus Business Cases

Some organizations use these terms interchangeably. Generally, the business case is a subset of a strategic plan. A business case generally addresses the "What?" and the "Why?" questions. A strategic plan also addresses the "How?"

Strategic Plans Versus Project Plans

The "How?" portion of a strategic plan can overlap with the project plan. So how do you know where to draw the line? The strategic plan includes enough detail to ensure everyone knows what you are trying to accomplish and what it will take to make it happen. Your project plan includes all the detail to actually make it happen.

Consider the difference between a travel guide and a travel map. A travel guide helps you determine where to go and what to see. That's your strategic plan. But when it comes time to actually go on the trip, you will need a road map to help decide which interstate and which exit to use. That's your project plan.

Elements of a Strategic Plan

How detailed should a strategic plan be? Only you and the people making the decisions about your project can answer this question. And the real answer may come in phases. For example, you may want to develop an extremely high-level cost-benefit analysis just to decide if it is worth the time and effort needed to build a more detailed business case. Then, when you are ready to ask for the funding and support, you create a more detailed plan.

Business Goals and Benefits

The foundation of any business strategy is: "Why?" In this case, why do you want e-learning?

In chapter 1, you learned about the advantages and disadvantages of e-learning. Now it is time to take those advantages and tie them to the issues and drivers in your organization. A training professional might first jump to the learning or training management benefits of e-learning, but it is best to start a few levels higher—with the business benefits.

Know What You Are Evaluating

When building the business case and reviewing the cost-benefit analysis, make sure you understand exactly WHAT you are evaluating:

- Are you comparing an e-learning course to no training at all?
- Are you comparing an e-learning course to the same course delivered in another format?
- Are you examining the benefits of computer-based training as well as the benefits of implementing a learning management system (LMS)?

The answers to these questions determine which parts of the analysis process you will use. For example, if you are looking to convert an existing training course to e-learning, should you include the benefits of conducting the training itself, or just the benefits of using the new format versus the old format? If you are considering the use of online courses as well as a learning management system, should you separate out the business cases or treat them as one?

Decide in advance exactly what decisions you and your organization need to make and exactly what benefits and what numbers will best help you make those decisions.

Tying E-Learning to Business Goals

To identify how e-learning ties into the organization's overall goals, ask yourself (and key stakeholders) the following questions:

Possible Elements in a Strategic Plan

Select the elements that relate to your decision-making process.

- ❏ Executive Summary
- ❏ Problem Statement
- ❏ Background
- ❏ Project Objectives
- ❏ Proposed Solution
- ❏ Cost-Benefit Analysis
- ❏ Alternative Solutions
- ❏ Recommendation
- ❏ Deliverables
- ❏ Quality Criteria
- ❏ Resource Requirements
- ❏ Known Constraints
- ❏ Estimated Timeline
- ❏ Proposed Budget
- ❏ Critical Success Factors
- ❏ Implementation Plan
- ❏ Evaluation Plan
- ❏ Management Plan
- ❏ Risks
- ❏ Risk Management Plan

- What business problems are we trying to solve?
- What business problems are we trying to prevent?
- What strategic goals does the organization have that e-learning would support?
- What strategic goals does the organization have that e-learning might hinder?

You will be in a better position to generate support and funding if you can show how the e-learning initiative is tied to the overall organizational strategy.

Benefits of the Training Program

If you are proposing a brand-new training program (regardless of format), you will want to analyze the benefits of conducting the program. This process is the same whether you are looking at classroom delivery or online delivery. Using a combination of interviews, brainstorming, and statistics, you'll want to create a list of anticipated benefits that include metrics such as:

- time saved
- productivity increased
- service increased
- turnover reduced
- quality increased
- safety violations reduced
- sales increased
- money saved
- liability decreased
- any other factors related to the project you are reviewing.

Benefits of the E-Learning Delivery Platform

Sometimes an e-learning project is not about the content—it is about the delivery method. Perhaps you have an effective classroom training program in place, but the question on the table is, "What are the business benefits for converting to a different delivery platform?"

Use the checklist in Figure 2-1 to see if you have some of the environmental factors that often make e-learning a good fit.

FIGURE 2-1: DO YOU NEED E-LEARNING?

	Yes	Some	No
1. Do you have a geographically dispersed workforce?			
2. Does your audience work in different time zones or on different shifts?			
3. Do you have to train on a subject frequently?			
4. Do you have people with low productivity or high error rates because they have to wait for the next training class to be offered?			
5. Do you have a large number of people to train?			
6. Do you have mandated training?			
7. Do you need to reach a lot of people very quickly (such as product knowledge for a new launch or a new legal requirement)?			
8. Do you need to train on complex information?			
9. Would it be useful for people to be able to go back and study a section again?			
10. Do you have a wide variety of preexisting knowledge on a subject (some learners are experienced, some are novices, and some in the middle)?			
11. Do different portions of your audience need slightly different information?			
12. Would you like people to be able to test out?			
13. Would your information benefit from video or animation (such as a moving diagram of how a manufacturing process works)?			
14. Would you like to provide the same level of training in less time?			

Note: There is no scoring for this checklist. If you say yes to just one question, and it's a big enough issue for you, then that alone may justify an e-learning project. Conversely, you may say yes to five or six questions, but another factor might make e-learning inappropriate. Use your answers to help you understand your business drivers.

For any question where you answered "yes," determine the benefits to you for using e-learning to deal with that issue. For example:

- If you have a geographically dispersed workforce, you might benefit from reduced travel costs, from providing training to smaller locations that currently don't receive the same training as the large offices, and from a consistent training message to all employees.

- If you have a wide variety of preexisting knowledge on a subject, you might benefit from less time spent in training overall if the experienced employees can skip the sections they already understand or can at least cover them at a quicker pace; or you could benefit from increased understanding by your inexperienced employees because they can take as much time as they need to really understand.

Continue through all items that apply to you until you have uncovered all the benefits you can think of.

Benefits of a Training Management System

If you are considering the use of a learning management system (LMS), learning content management system (LCMS), or other administrative software, continue the process by identifying the benefits of such a system. These are some potential benefits:

- reduced data entry time
- increased protection against liability
- reduced time needed to create compliance documentation
- increased training completion due to automated registrations, reminders, and exception reports.

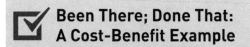

Been There; Done That: A Cost-Benefit Example

Consider that using an e-learning format will reduce the amount of time your sales people will spend in training when they could be meeting with potential clients.

- To what degree? How much more time will they be able to spend on sales activities?
- At what cost or savings? If a salesperson is selling x hours a month more, how much is that likely to increase sales?

Through research and interviews, you determine that the new format will save five hours a month. That increased sales activity is likely to lead to 0.5 more sales per month with a company average order of $6,000. There are 35 sales reps.

Monthly benefit = 0.5 sales x $6,000 x 35 people = $105,000 increased sales per month.

Cost-Benefit Analysis

The core of your business case will be the cost-benefit analysis. This can be a formal, quantitative analysis including a complete return on investment (ROI) statement or an informal, qualitative approach that considers tangible as well as intangible benefits.

This section focuses on the cost-benefit analysis and ROI estimates for the use of a self-paced e-learning course. If you want to conduct a similar assessment on the need for a particular training program, there are many excellent resources available to help you. For now, assume the training need has been justified, and the use of an e-learning delivery platform is what is being considered.

Quantifying Benefits

Perhaps the hardest part of building a business case is trying to quantify the impact of all the benefits you just identified. Some might be easy to quantify, such as reduced travel costs. Some may be almost impossible to quantify, such as increased morale. Most, however, fall somewhere in between.

Most benefits can be quantified by asking two questions: To what degree? At what cost or savings? These factors, when combined with the number of people affected, can give you a numerical value for the benefit.

Answering the two core questions may be challenging. Look to other departments to see if they already have metrics for some of the issues. For example, does the human resources department know your current turnover rate as well as the cost to hire a new employee? Does the production department have numbers about the error rates of new employees versus those who have completed training? Does the customer service department know the cost of a dropped call?

Most likely, you will come up with some benefits that you cannot quantify. Then you will have to decide how you want to deal with them. Some organizations choose not to include them if they cannot be quantified. Others create a separate section that deals with "intangibles."

Quantifying Costs

To determine if the benefits are worth it, you will want to create a high-level estimate for the overall cost of the program.

Direct Program Costs

Direct program costs can be challenging to determine early on in an e-learning project because you haven't yet made a lot of the decisions that will go into your ultimate project budget. At this point, you will want to come up with some estimated high-level numbers about what you will need to spend. Refer to chapter 3 for help in determining your direct program costs.

Indirect Program Costs

The most common indirect cost for a training program would be an opportunity cost. For example, what could your money and people be doing if they weren't doing this? What is the cost of that missed opportunity?

So in this case, what would your training team, your SMEs, or your IT team be doing if they were not working on this project?

Comparison Methods

Once you have identified and quantified your costs and benefits, you can evaluate the business case.

Comparing Costs to Costs

If you are looking at converting an existing classroom program to an online delivery format, you would simply compare the cost of each in a side-by-side comparison. To do this, you will want to estimate the shelf life of the materials and project the costs out for that period of time.

FIGURE 2-2: SAMPLE COST COMPARISON FOR AN ORIENTATION PROGRAM

Classroom Delivery	
Costs for a six-hour class of 15 people every month for three years.	
Materials	$5,400
Instructor's salary	$6,480
Refreshments	$5,940
Learners' wages @ $10/hr	$32,400
Total cost for three years	$50,220

Online Delivery	
*Costs for a three-hour online course used for three years.**	
Contract development	$45,000
Learners' wages @ $10/hr	$16,200
Total cost for three years	$61,200

* An online course typically takes half the time of the equivalent instructor-led course.

FIGURE 2-3: SAMPLE COST COMPARISON FOR NEW PRODUCT TRAINING (INCLUDING INTANGIBLES)

Classroom Delivery	
Costs for a one-day class for 35 people.	
Contract development	$8,000
Materials	$350
Instructor's salary	$500
Facilities	$750
Refreshments	$450
Travel (mileage)	$850
Lodging (for four reps)	$300
Lost sales while in training and transit	$210,000
Total cost	$221,200

Online Delivery	
Costs for a three-hour online course.	
Contract development	$45,000
Materials	$175
Lost sales while in training (training taken during non-productive times such as flights or while waiting for meetings)	$0
10% reduced sales of new product for first two months because opportunity for practice was not provided	$71,400
Total cost	$116,575

Comparing Costs to Benefits

Rather than comparing the two sets of costs, you could simply look at the costs versus the benefits of the one delivery option.

FIGURE 2-4: COSTS VERSUS BENEFITS FOR A LEARNING MANAGEMENT SYSTEM

Benefits Over Three Years		Costs Over Three Years	
Elimination of 1.5 FTE training assistants*	$189,000	Hardware upgrades	$12,000
		Software license	$35,000
		Implementation and testing	$15,000
		0.25 FTE LMS administrator	$67,500
Total cost for three years	$189,000	Total cost for three years	$129,500

*FTE = full-time equivalent

Calculation Methods

There are a number of different ways to present your bottom-line numbers. Cost-benefit ratio and return on investment are two of the most common.

Cost-benefit ratio:

Financial Benefits ÷ Total Cost of Training = Cost-Benefit Ratio

Example: $189,000 ÷ $129,500 = $1.46

This means that for every dollar invested, it will return $1.46.

Different organizations have different opinions about what an acceptable cost-benefit ratio is. Some would say that anything over the break-even point (1.0) is worth doing. Others would say that there is not enough benefit to be worth the trouble unless the benefit is a certain amount over 1.0.

Return on Investment (ROI):

(Total Benefits - Total Costs) ÷ Total Costs x 100 = ROI

Example: ($189,000 - $129,500) ÷ $129,500 x 100 = 46%

This calculation gives a similar result as the cost-benefit ratio, but in different terms. This shows that the ROI is 46 percent of every dollar spent for training: 46 cents. As with the cost-benefit ratio, different organizations have different opinions regarding an acceptable ROI.

Generating Support

An e-learning project requires the support of many groups throughout the organization. Gathering this support and troubleshooting any issues will help your project flow more smoothly.

Identify Stakeholders

Because e-learning projects tend to be more expensive and more involved than a typical training project, you will often need to involve more people than you are used to. Take the time to figure out who they are before you need them—and before they find you!

Use the Stakeholder Worksheet to identify the different groups who may want to have a say in how the project is handled. It is better to involve too many people than to forget someone with important input.

FIGURE 2-5: STAKEHOLDER WORKSHEET

Who are they?	What do they want?	Why do they want it?

 Been There; Done That: A Surprise Stakeholder

A medium-sized financial services firm was making good progress on its first e-learning initiative—a two-hour overview of the company and the industry. When the online draft was posted for internal review, the marketing department took a look and discovered that the interface was not using the company's standard for web fonts or the correct shade of navy blue.

These would have been easy changes to make during the design phase. But since production had already begun, the changes were more expensive. The moral of the story: Get everyone involved early!!

Recognize Priorities, Motives, Obstacles

Now that you've found your stakeholders, don't be surprised if they don't all jump up and down for joy about your new project. Take the time to think about the priorities and motives each group might be dealing with and the obstacles that might arise. For example:

- Upper management may be hesitant because previous IT projects did not result in the benefits promised.

- Training management may agree with the business case on paper, but they don't want to be responsible personally for the risks.

- Trainers may resist because they secretly wonder if their jobs will go away or if they will understand the new technology.

- The information technology department may pose objections because they are already overworked, and this would be one more system to support.

- Line managers may consider this just another management fad that will take up their time.

- Employees may be uncomfortable with the technology and disappointed that they don't get the "time off" to go to the training classes, which they enjoy.

When building the business case, you took the time to analyze the benefits, costs, and risks of the project from your perspective. Now take the time to examine the project honestly from everyone else's perspective. This will help you overcome resistance, remove potential obstacles for these groups, and create a cohesive team.

Educate on Features, Benefits, and Costs

From this point until the formal project sign-off, your job is communication. Use your strategic plan, benefit analysis, and other information to educate the key stakeholders on what you are trying to do and why. But also be sure to listen to everyone's input as well. Work hard to distinguish what is a fear and what is a legitimate concern. Be prepared to make compromises or adjustments to ensure that everyone's needs are met.

Summary

You may be under pressure to jump into a project quickly so you can be up and running right away. Conversely, you may also be under pressure to document and prove the ROI mathematically well before you know enough to make that kind of determination. In the end, a balanced approach will help you ensure that your e-learning project has a strong justification, a feasible plan, and a supportive team. As you do so, keep these key points in mind:

- Understand what you are trying to accomplish and why.

- Link project goals to overall business goals.

- Identify and quantify benefits.

- Identify high-level costs.

- Calculate the return.

- Identify key stakeholders and their motivations.

- Build support.

3

MANAGING AN E-LEARNING PROJECT

Every training development project requires strong management skills. But because an e-learning project generally takes more time, costs more money, and involves more people, an emphasis on proper management is even more important.

From defining and managing the project to budgeting and working with vendors, you'll want to stay on top of all the details to make sure your project is delivered on time, on track, and on budget.

The Project Management Model and the ADDIE Model

The ADDIE model (analyze, design, develop, implement, evaluate) is widely used to manage training development. While the use of this model helps ensure that you have high-quality, effective training, it doesn't necessarily mean the project itself will be run smoothly and efficiently.

Therefore, a combination of the ADDIE model and the project management model can help you create great training while keeping your project on track. The ADDIE model helps you create an effective course, while the project management model helps you run an efficient project. You'll learn more about the ADDIE model in the second half of this book.

FIGURE 3-1: THE ADDIE MODEL VERSUS THE PROJECT MANAGEMENT MODEL

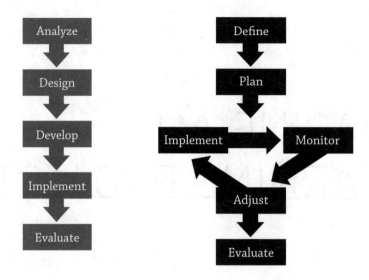

Define the Project

The definition phase of a project is very similar to the analysis phase of the ADDIE model—you are trying to find out what needs to be accomplished. From a project management standpoint, you'll want to make sure you know four main things:

- what you are trying to do
- why you are trying to do it
- who your customers or stakeholders are
- what success looks like.

 The Great Debate: Traditional or Agile Project Management?

In recent years, the traditional project management model has come under criticism for being too rigid and for taking too long. Some e-learning project managers are moving more toward Agile project management techniques (such as LLAMA), which allow for more changes as a project manager learns more about the project.

Steps for Defining Your Project

Traditional training analysis does not always consider the business environment in which the project needs to take place—that's where project management comes in.

Create Project Goals and Objectives

In addition to the specific training goals for your course (see chapter 6), you want to ensure that you understand (and everyone agrees upon) the reasons why this project is necessary. Think of it as the problem needing to be solved. For example:

- to prepare employees in all 35 locations for the rollout of the new customer-relationship software in April

- to provide the same training opportunities for supervisors in our remote locations as the supervisors in our home office.

Understand Drivers

It may seem obvious, but make sure everyone is clear about what everyone's motivation is. For example, if your company is starting e-learning because the new CEO thinks it's cool, then you might approach your project one way. If you are starting e-learning because you want better records because of a painful loss on a court case, you might manage the project differently. The drivers around the project dictate how much support you get (and keep), what kind of decisions to make, and what kind of trade-offs might be necessary.

Identify Constraints

While it is generally too early to create a detailed schedule and budget, you may be able to identify high-level resource and time constraints. For example, some e-learning projects might have an end-of-the-year goal that is fairly arbitrary—the goal is there to have something to shoot for. But another project might have an end-of-the-year goal because of a new product launch or a grant-funding deadline. Other constraints might be a hiring freeze or lack of project funding. Understanding your constraints will help you better manage the entire project.

Deliverables for the Project Definition Phase

Through interviews, negotiations, and brainstorming sessions, you will create a vision for the project. This vision should be documented, shared with key stakeholders, and signed off by the project sponsor. This documentation may come in the form of a project charter, scope of work, or project definition statement.

These documents can take any shape or format. If your organization already works with some of these documents on other projects, consider borrowing their formats.

Project Definition Questions

Problem

- What are we trying to do?
- What are we really trying to do?
- What problems are we trying to solve?
- What caused the problems?
- What client needs will be satisfied?
- What are the benefits?

Customers and Stakeholders Statement

- Who is this for?
- Who else is this for?
- Who else needs to be happy for this to be considered a success?
- Who else might want some input?
- Who else might be affected?

Objectives and Scope

- What is the desired outcome? (multiple answers)
- What is the gap between what you want and what you have?
- How will you know you have achieved the desired result?
- What will be different that you can see, hear, touch, measure?
- Which quality criteria are "must do," "should do," and "nice to do"?
- What "extras" might the stakeholders be unknowingly expecting?
- Will successful completion give rise to other needs?
- What does not have to be done?
- I'm sure there's something else—what is it?

Constraints and Obstacles

- What prevents us from achieving the objective or makes it difficult?
- What resource and time constraints exist?
- What is the driver? Does everyone agree?

Additional Issues

- What other needs might be present? Consider department, manager, client, company, and personal.

Sample Scope of Work for E-Learning Course Development

- Overview
- Project goals
- Audience
- Tasks to be performed
- Roles and responsibilities
- Technical specifications
- Deliverables
- Success criteria
- Deadline

Dive Deeper

Fundamentals of Project Management by James P. Lewis

Plan the Project

The planning phase of the project management life cycle corresponds closely to the design phase of the ADDIE model. So while you are designing what the courses should look like, you will need to plan what the project will look like.

This is once again the chicken-and-egg scenario. It will be difficult to finalize decisions about level of effort, schedule, and budget until you know what the design will look like. (For example, if the course will include audio or a randomized bank of questions, you will have a higher development effort than if you didn't include either of those.) At the same time, you can't really wait until the design is done to create your project plan, because the design phase is part of what needs to be managed!

Most e-learning managers start out with a high-level plan based on early information, and then revise the plan at the end of the design phase. If you are going to use this approach, make sure the stakeholders know that the first plan is tentative.

A project plan generally contains these elements: task list and schedule; resources (money, staff, equipment); and risks (along with mitigation strategies and contingencies).

The plan can be developed using a project management tool such as Microsoft Project or with regular desktop applications such as Microsoft Word or Excel. Additional information on budgets, staff, and schedules is provided later in this chapter.

FIGURE 3-2: SAMPLE PROJECT MANAGEMENT SCHEDULE

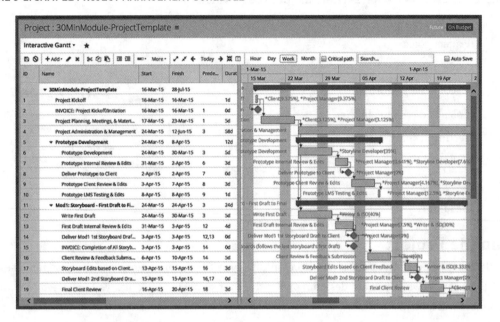

Tips From the Pros: Possible Project Risks

Consider these possible risks for an e-learning project:

- unavailability of subject matter experts (SMEs)
- unavailability of IT resources
- managers not giving their employees the time to take the courses
- possible incompatibility of systems
- low bandwidth
- resistance from training team on switch to e-learning
- changing content.

Implement, Monitor, and Adjust the Project

In the ADDIE model, implementation means actually launching the training. In the project management model, implementation means *doing* the work. This can mean the design, development, and implementation of a training project.

To manage the project effectively, you should have a solid system for tracking progress, such as which module is being built and which one is being reviewed (as shown in Figure 3.3), and dealing with issues, such as missing content, open questions, or technical implementation concerns (as shown in Figure 3.4). Because e-learning projects are generally more complex than a classroom training project, you may want to use more formal methods of tracking.

Status meetings, status reports, and project management software can all help you stay on top of things. Perhaps a simple spreadsheet posted on a shared drive can help you keep everything under control. Be sure to build this project management time into your schedule and development estimates.

FIGURE 3-3: DEVELOPMENT TRACKING SPREADSHEET

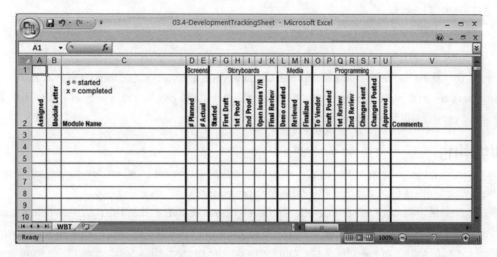

FIGURE 3-4: ISSUES TRACKING SPREADSHEET

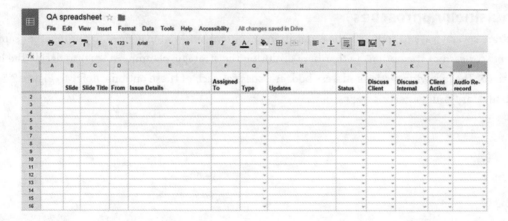

Evaluate the Project

Chapter 12 covers the evaluation of the training. But at the end of a project, take the time to evaluate the process as well. Hold a debriefing session and discuss what worked well and what didn't in terms of:

- team structure
- schedule
- budget
- communication
- handling issues
- teamwork
- customer service.

Conducting these sessions takes discipline. Usually when a project is finished, you are already starting your next project. Build the time into your initial schedule to conduct this project evaluation. Every subsequent project will be stronger for it.

Budgeting

Which came first, the chicken or the egg? A similar question can be asked when developing an e-learning budget, "Which comes first: the budget or the specifications?"

It is challenging to put together a detailed budget without knowing what the courses will look like and how they will be developed. Yet it can be a waste of time to get all the specifications you need without knowing for sure that you even have the money to do the project. This section outlines some general guidelines for you to consider when putting together your budget.

Acquisition Approaches

There are several ways to approach the acquisition of content, and you may need to put together sample budgets for each of the options (either here or during the strategic planning stages) to decide the best way to go. The following sections address budget issues for each of these options. Refer to Figure 3.5 for nonbudgetary issues affecting acquisitions.

FIGURE 3-5: REASONS FOR DIFFERENT ACQUISITION APPROACHES

OFF-THE-SHELF COURSEWARE

☐ You want to get up and running quickly.

☐ You would rather spread your costs out over time.

☐ You do not have a high volume of users.

☐ You are looking for a package deal including LMS functionality.

☐ You are looking for topics that are not industry or company specific.

CUSTOM DEVELOPMENT: CONTRACTING OUT

☐ You have no e-learning experience on your team.

☐ You expect the workload to be short lived or inconsistent.

☐ You don't want to take people's focus away from other efforts.

☐ It is easier to find consulting dollars than employee dollars.

☐ You don't want to spend the time or money needed to develop a team.

CUSTOM DEVELOPMENT: DEVELOPING INTERNALLY

☐ You want full control over your content.

☐ You expect a long-term, consistent production effort.

☐ You are able to bring on additional staff.

☐ You are able to provide adequate training for your staff.

Types of Expenses

Development Tools

Development tools come in many shapes, sizes . . . and prices. You can find out more about the tools themselves in chapter 4, but for now, include the cost of some or all of these tools in your budget if you will be developing courseware internally.

Course-Authoring Tools

Course-authoring tools are used to assemble the courseware. Some tools, such as Udutu, are free or open source. A few tools can cost more than $10,000. However, most of the major e-learning authoring tools, such as Adobe Captivate, Articulate Studio, Articulate Storyline, and Trivantis Lectora, cost between $800 and $2,500.

 Tips from the Pros: The Real Cost

Be careful about picking a tool just because it is cheaper. It may not meet your needs instructionally or technically. In addition, the long-term cost of ownership may be higher if it takes your people much more time to develop content in that tool.

Course Element Tools

In addition to the software you use to assemble the course, you may want specialized software for specific elements. These packages can range from $100 to over $1,000. You may want several—or you may not need any. It all depends upon how you design your course and what features are already available in your authoring tool. Here are some examples:

- graphics software such as Photoshop Elements
- software simulation tools such as Captivate or Camtasia
- assessment tools such as QuestionMark Perception
- game development software such as Raptivity.

You may also want to budget for a graphics library of some sort. You might purchase a subscription from companies, such as istockphoto or eLearning Brothers, or plan to pay per image as needed.

Pricing Models: Installed Versus Cloud Based

Some development tools are available as an installed solution, which means you buy the software, install it on your computer, and use it as long as you like (similar to your word processing or spreadsheet software). Prices in this section reflect this model.

Some tools, however, are available as a hosted or cloud-based solution, such as dominKnow by Claro. With this type of solution you don't own the software, but instead use it for a specified period of time (usually one to three years) and access it from the web. When you cancel the agreement, you can no longer use the software. If you are considering a cloud-based solution, make sure you understand all the fees involved. Some companies have a fee to use the software and then additional fees each time the course is accessed.

The Great Debate: Cloud-Based vs. Installed Software

Which is better: cloud-based software or installed software? Here are some factors to consider.

Cost: In general, the initial cost of ownership is lower with a cloud-based solution in which you pay a little bit every year, but total cost of ownership is often lower with an installed solution if you plan to use it for more than three years. With cloud-based solutions, you typically get all upgrades as part of your subscription. With installed software, you typically have to pay another fee for each upgrade, which can often cost as much as 50 percent of the original price.

Availability: When you use cloud-based software, you can only use it when you have Internet access. And if that Internet access is slow, it will take you longer to do your work. With installed software, you don't need to worry about that possible downtime. However, with installed software, you can only work on your projects if you are on a computer that has it installed. With cloud-based software, you can do your work from any computer with Internet access.

Longevity: When you buy installed software, you pay for it once. Unless you choose to upgrade, you can use that license for as long as current technology allows. The software company could even go out of business, and you could still use the software. With cloud-based solutions, you typically have to renew (pay) every year. If your funding runs out or if the software company goes out of business, you lose access to your software (including your ability to maintain existing courses).

Other Technology

You may need to budget for other technology needs that are part of the overall e-learning landscape at your organization, such as:

- LMS and learning record stores (LRS): to launch and track your training
- learning content management systems (LCMS): to help manage reusability of course assets
- synchronous platforms: for webinars
- social media/collaboration platforms: for discussion forums and other collaborative activities.

Internal Team Members or Contractors

Depending on how your company's budgeting process works, you may need to include line items for all the people working on the design and development. Even if you are outsourcing development, some of your internal team resources will be needed to manage the project and the vendor. There is additional information to help you determine your project staffing needs later in this chapter.

Most people would pay between $12,000 and $30,000 per course hour.

When calculating your budget, you may need to include salaries, overhead costs, and benefits for each team member, possible overtime, and SME time.

Again, your budget will have to reflect your company's philosophies. In some situations, you may also need to include in your budget the wages for the learners while they are taking the courses.

Outsourcing Development

Asking how much it costs to outsource development is like asking how much it costs to buy a car. The answer depends upon what you want.

At the low end, you can pay a few hundred to a few thousand dollars for someone to convert a Power-Point presentation online or to put a simple series of text-based web pages online when all the content is already put together. At the high end, you could pay $50,000 and up per finished course hour if you want extensive simulations, high-quality video, or 3-D animations.

Most people can expect to pay between $12,000 and $30,000 per finished course hour. The major variables include:

- **The condition of the content**—Expect to pay less if all the material is written out somewhere; expect to pay more if all the material is in someone's head.

- **The level of interactions and questions**—Expect to pay less for straightforward rollovers and standard question types; expect to pay more for branching scenarios and elaborate simulations.

- **The media used**—Expect to pay less for stock photography and video you provide; expect to pay more for custom graphics, animations, professional voice talent, and shooting or editing any video.

- **Special programming requirements**—Expect to pay less for a template-driven course with preset options; expect to pay more for special requirements such as custom learning paths, section 508 compliance, or anything else "really cool" you can think of.

- **Review cycles**—If not managed properly, review cycles can take longer and cost more than the initial development. The number of people involved, number of reviews conducted, and number of changes allowed will all affect your costs.

Other Costs

Gather your best brainstormers together to make sure you are considering all your costs. Because each project is different, each budget will be different. Try to conduct your analysis (chapter 5) before committing to your budget. You may uncover additional costs:

- video footage
- professional voice talent for audio

- implementation and promotional costs such as a logo or marketing materials
- training for your team in e-learning design
- anything else you can think of.

Resources

If you are creating an internal development team, you will want to make some important decisions about who should be involved—and to what degree.

Skills Needed

Regardless of how big or small your development effort is, an internal development team needs to possess certain skills. For a large development team, you may need several people for each role. For a smaller team, you may need to find one person who can wear all or most of the hats, perhaps supported by contractors or vendors to fill the gaps. You may need to hire someone who already has the needed skill or send a team member to specialized training to learn a new skill.

 Tips From the Pros: Budgeting for E-Learning Development

E-learning development takes various specialized talents. Based on your course design, you may need to budget for these areas:

instructional design	project management
graphic design	proofreading
subject matter expertise	voice talent
quality assurance testing	editing
research	audio recording and editing
online instruction	programming/course assembly
writing	video production and editing.

FIGURE 3-6: SAMPLE BUDGETING WORKSHEET

Item	Per Unit Cost	Number of Units	Total Cost
Development tools			
Authoring tools			
Graphics library			
Audio recording equipment			
Training on new tools			
Staff (internal or contract)			
Course developers			
Proofreaders			
Programmers			
Consultant for first course			
Project manager			
SMEs			
Learners' wages during course			
IT costs			
Additional servers			
Additional computer kiosks			
Headsets			
New training dept. workstation			
Help-desk support			
Additional costs			
Program promotion and launch			
Evaluation expenses			
Course-update costs			
TOTAL			

Timelines and Development Ratios

When creating initial estimates for first-time projects, you will probably need to rely on industry averages. According to the Chapman Alliance, a basic one-hour course might take 80 hours to create. For high-end courses or development that involves full analysis and content gathering, you may spend over 500 hours for one hour of courseware.

FIGURE 3-7: DEVELOPMENT RATIOS

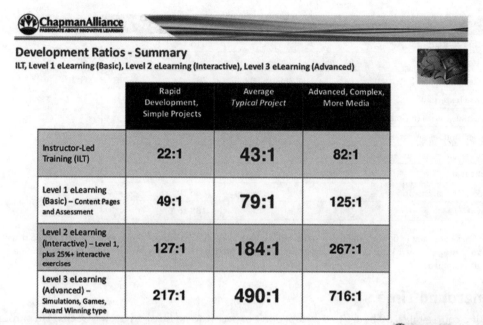

	Rapid Development, Simple Projects	Average *Typical Project*	Advanced, Complex, More Media
Instructor-Led Training (ILT)	22:1	43:1	82:1
Level 1 eLearning (Basic) – Content Pages and Assessment	49:1	79:1	125:1
Level 2 eLearning (Interactive) – Level 1, plus 25%+ interactive exercises	127:1	184:1	267:1
Level 3 eLearning (Advanced) – Simulations, Games, Award Winning type	217:1	490:1	716:1

Development Ratios - Summary
ILT, Level 1 eLearning (Basic), Level 2 eLearning (Interactive), Level 3 eLearning (Advanced)

Research data collected: September 2010, by Chapman Alliance

Used with permission of Chapman Alliance.

The biggest variables surrounding how long it will take to create a course are the same variables that affect the cost of a course:

- condition of the content
- level of interactions and questions
- media used
- special programming requirements
- review cycles.

The best way to estimate the timeline for any project is to break it down into little pieces. The task of estimating a whole project may seem daunting, but you might have a better "feel" when estimating individual sections of the project. Based on what you know about your project, your team, and your environment, you can design a chart similar to the one in Figure 3-8.

FIGURE 3-8: SAMPLE DEVELOPMENT HOURS RATIO CHART

Task	Ratio to Develop
Gather content	6 to 1
Write storyboards	30 to 1
Review and revise (internal)	20 to 1
Revise (external)	10 to 1
Assemble course (including media)	70 to 1
Review and revise (internal)	20 to 1
Review and revise (external)	10 to 1
Subtotal	**166 to 1**
Project management	Add 10%
Total	**183 to 1**

NOTE: These are sample figures. Your own ratios will be based on what you know about your project and your team. As you begin your project, you'll keep detailed records about the production process so you can create more accurate estimates for future development.

Turnaround Time

Even if a course takes 80 hours to develop, don't expect it to be finished in two weeks. Turnaround time will be based largely on:

- **The percentage of time each team member can devote to the project**—Ask yourself how much time your team spends on other projects, administrative tasks, and in departmental meetings, among other duties.

- **The number of people on the project**—Each time the project passes from one person to another, you are likely to lose a little time.

- **Your review cycles**—Each time your customers (internal or external) or SMEs review the course, you may need to add two more weeks. At the beginning of a project you may hear that two-day turnaround times are promised, but that may not happen.

- **The experience level of the people on the project**—For an established team that works well together, a typical one-hour course may take eight weeks to turn around. But a new team may need twice that amount of time.

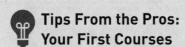

Tips From the Pros: Your First Courses

Your first few courses will take considerably longer than later courses. Many design and technology decisions need to be made; many processes need to be established; and much organizational coordination needs to take place.

The analysis and design phases for your first course might take between six weeks and three months— even more if you run into obstacles or if you need to first implement an enterprise-wide system such as an LMS in a large company.

Working With Vendors

An e-learning project may include vendors to provide software, hardware, consulting, or development. Selecting these vendors is an important decision and might best be treated as its own project.

Caveat emptor: Let the buyer beware. A lot of money is being spent in the e-learning marketplace. Fortunately, there are a lot of reputable, qualified vendors who do a great job. But then there are some who just aren't very good at what they do. And, unfortunately, there are a handful who are just in the marketplace to cash in.

Part of what makes the selection of an e-learning vendor challenging is the fact that you may not know enough to assess when a vendor is good, operating outside of his or her expertise, or is about to rip you off.

Your best protection against picking a bad vendor is doing your homework: making sure you know what you do and do not want and taking a systematic approach to vendor selection. Your best protection against having a project go sour because of a vendor is to make sure you manage the relationship formally.

RFIs and RFPs

Requests for information (RFIs) and requests for proposal (RFPs) are the two primary tools you can use to select a vendor of any kind.

In general, an RFI is used for preliminary research to help you identify which vendors offer the type of product or service you want and what the general costs and turnaround times would be. RFIs are useful when you are in initial planning stages. Perhaps you don't know exactly what you want, but you want to get at least a general idea of what is out there so that you can sketch out a preliminary budget. This can help you decide if you even want to move forward with the full planning process.

 Tips from the Pros: Tips for Creating an RFI

You may end up wading through pages and pages of marketing language trying to search for answers to your questions. To make your job simpler, be very specific about how you want them to respond:

- Provide a form with simple yes-and-no questions. (Example: Is your system Section 508 compliant?)
- Set a page limit.
- Provide an outline for them to use when writing their response.
- Let them know that an average price or price range is required.

Creating an RFI

RFIs are fairly simple to put together because they are based on general project goals, rather than detailed specifications. Create a document that outlines:

- information about your company and audience
- what you are trying to accomplish
- the type of product or service you are looking for
- any specifications you already know
- how you want them to respond.

For example, you might create a simple document explaining that:

- You are a small manufacturing firm with 1,250 employees in eight offices throughout the Northeast.
- You are looking at offering online safety training for all employees (you can list the specific topics you are interested in).
- You want a vendor with existing courseware that you can license.
- You would like their system to pull from your ADP employee database and provide reports on completion and test scores.
- The courses cannot require audio because the computer workstations do not have soundcards or speakers.
- You would like them to respond via email within two weeks and provide their list of titles, operating requirements, tracking capabilities, a link to a sample course, and an average, nonbinding price for the type of arrangement you are seeking.

The entire document may only be a few pages long. Remember, you are just trying to gather information to help you plan.

Sample RFP Outline for Custom Course Development

Background
    Company Profile
    Audience Profile
    Project Goals
Statement of Work
    Course Length
    Course Features and Functions
        Interface
        Menus and Navigation
        Interactions
        Additional Features
    Media Elements
    LMS Integration
    Responsibilities
        Client
        Vendor
    Technical Requirements
    Review Cycles
    Deliverables
        Major Milestones
        Project Schedule
Terms
    Payment Terms
    Ownership
    Confidentiality
Instructions to Proposer
    Proposal Contents
        Cost
        Experience
        Technical
        Samples
        References
    Submission Guidelines
Selection Criteria
Contact Information
Appendix A
    Course Module Breakdown
Appendix B
    Example of Existing Content

Creating an RFP

RFPs are more formal documents that specifically list what you want and help the vendor provide a specific, binding proposal. While putting an RFP together can take a lot of time and effort, it will pay off. Using a formal proposal process helps you:

- **Increase competition**—You can send your requests to any number of companies to increase your chances of getting a great vendor and a good deal.

- **Ensure apples-to-apples comparisons**—To really evaluate the differences between vendors, it helps to compare the same thing. Using a formal proposal process ensures that you are comparing like products and services.

- **Clarify your own needs**—The act of writing the RFP is valuable in and of itself. Even if you never send the RFP out, you will have learned a lot about your project and what you are trying to accomplish.

- **Formalize the agreement**—The RFP and the resulting proposal spell out the details of the relationship. Often the final contract will refer to the RFP or the proposal, rather than repeat all the details. Having everything spelled out in writing helps eliminate surprises.

An RFP asks for a specific, binding proposal. In order for a vendor to respond accurately, you will need to provide a lot of detail. It can be very time consuming to create an RFP, which may range anywhere from five to 500 pages! (Most projects would need about 10 to 30 pages.) The good news is that if you've done your homework in planning your project, your statement of work and requirements document can easily be converted to an RFP.

But what if you don't know all the details about what you want, and that's part of what you want the vendor to help you with? You have two options.

One option is to treat the analysis and design phases as a separate project with a separate contract, price, and schedule. This works well with custom development projects. You could end up with a requirements definition, design document, and about 30 to 60 minutes of content. From there, you create a separate RFP and contract for the full development based on what you have learned.

Another option is to work with the vendors to help you determine what you need and help you write the RFP. But be careful. Many salespeople are trained to convince you they have exactly what you need. If you go this route, make sure you talk to several vendors to get different perspectives.

Major RFP elements will be the same regardless of the type of project:

- company background
- project overview
- terms
- scope of work or product requirements (pulled from your internal documents)
- instructions for submission.

Specific elements will vary based on the type of project (LMS selection or custom course development, for example).

The most common problems with RFPs include lack of input from all parties (such as IT), sketchy details about the project and what is expected, and unclear guidelines about how the vendor should respond. To help reduce these problems, get all major stakeholders to sign off on the request and have someone who is not close to the project review the document to make sure your RFP is clear.

Evaluating Vendor Responses

The review process may consist of reading proposals, reviewing demos, listening to presentations, calling references, even evaluating prototypes created just for you.

The best time to think about how you want to evaluate the vendors is when you are creating the RFP. You want to make sure you ask them for everything you want to know. Do not assume they will provide samples and references—ask.

Decide who should be involved in the selection process. Do you want an end user to review the demo? Do you want an IT representative to confirm the technical details and ask any follow-up questions? Do you want the legal department to review the terms and even the courseware?

Determine your selection criteria and rank them. You may have "must-have," "should-have," and "nice-to-have" criteria. Then create a spreadsheet or chart to evaluate each vendor according to the criteria.

Working With Vendors

Get Everything in Writing

If the salesperson makes promises over the phone, make sure they get in the contract. During development, always keep your design document and other guidelines up-to-date with anything the vendor promised doing.

Put Protections in the Contract for You

If the vendor supplies the contract, make sure you are protected. Are there cancellation and privacy clauses for you or just the vendor? Are there late fees if you do not pay on time, but no penalties if the vendor delivers late?

FIGURE 3-9: SAMPLE EVALUATION SPREADSHEET FOR OFF-THE-SHELF CONTENT

Criteria	Points	Vendor A	Vendor B
Course offerings	150	100	150
Course quality	200	175	130
LMS capabilities	100	75	75
Company stability	125	75	100
Project management ability	50	50	40
Customer service	100	100	80
Technical support	75	75	40
Price	200	175	100
TOTAL	**1,000**	**825**	**715**

 ## Been There; Done That: A Bankruptcy Horror Story

A customer had a great relationship with a vendor. Together they created a series of video-streaming courses on management topics. The vendor hosted the courses for a fee. A year later, the vendor went bankrupt and its assets were sold at auction. Unfortunately, the vendor kept the copyright and source code for the courses, so they, too, were sold at auction. The new vendor got all the content, but was not bound to the original terms of the contract. The customer then had to negotiate with the new company for the right to access its own courses.

- Provide an outline for them to use when writing their response.
- Let them know that an average price or price range is required.

Know What Happens if the Vendor Goes Bankrupt

The e-learning world is not 100 percent stable. If your vendor goes out of business, find out what will happen to your courses, your content, your private company information. Put provisions in the contract that protect you.

Keep a Single Point of Contact

Negotiate for a single project manager and try to interview that person before the contract is signed. The salesperson may be great, but that isn't the person who will be helping you day in and day out.

Keep Ownership of Copyright, Data, and Source Code

For custom-developed courses, make sure you retain copyright and negotiate to keep the source code. (Some vendors may want you to pay extra for the source code.)

Understand the Scope Change Process

You've signed off on the storyboards and the vendor is halfway done building the first online draft. You get word that the very policy you are training on has just changed. How much will it cost to have those changes made to your course?

Make sure you fully understand when you will be signing off on what, as well as how much changes will cost after the fact. Be sure to manage the change process on your end. The farther into a project you make changes, the more expensive it will be. Take the time to conduct thorough reviews so needed changes don't come back to bite you later.

Have Regular Progress Updates

Whether you use written reports or weekly conference calls, take the initiative to stay on top of the milestones.

Make Payments Milestone Based Instead of Time Based

If the contract has calendar-based milestones, you could end up paying for deliverables that haven't been delivered! And always hold the last chunk of money (10 to 25 percent) until everything is delivered. (Be good to your vendor, though. If there are long schedule delays that are your fault, find a way to pay the vendor for work completed.)

Be Wary of Proprietary Code

If a vendor uses proprietary software, you may forever be tied to that vendor and may not be able to change your courses or move them to a different platform.

Be a Good Customer

Customers tell horror stories about vendors. But vendors tell horror stories about customers, too. Be respectful of their time and efforts by honoring your end of all the agreements. Be realistic when expecting them to make changes and corrections because you've changed your mind or you missed something.

Summary

Great e-learning projects don't just happen. They are expertly defined, planned, implemented, and evaluated. By adding project management tools to your toolbox, you will increase the efficiency of the process and the quality of the end product.

4

TOOLS OF THE TRADE

Newcomers to the world of e-learning can be easily overwhelmed by all the technology decisions they have to make, the number of choices available, and the unfamiliar terminology. This chapter describes the tools necessary to create or manage a self-paced e-learning program.

This information works in conjunction with the material in later chapters: Chapter 5, covering the analysis phase, helps you define your company's hardware and software needs. Chapters 6, 7, and 8, discussing the design phase of the project, help you determine what specific features you want to incorporate into your courses. Making these decisions helps you understand what the best tools are to meet your needs.

Authoring Tools

What is an authoring tool? Definitions may vary based on whom you ask. For the purposes of this book, an authoring tool is the software you use to assemble the course. It is the tool you would use to place all your course elements (such as text, graphics, and questions) and turn individual screens into a complete course (with pages, navigation, menus, and buttons).

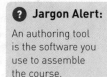

❓ Jargon Alert:

An authoring tool is the software you use to assemble the course.

Authoring tools have a variety of features, come in a wide range of prices, and require different levels of skill. Some tools are very simple to use with templates, wizards, and features that work just like common business software such as Word or PowerPoint. Other tools allow for greater design flexibility but are more difficult to learn—some even require programming knowledge.

Selecting the right tool involves consideration of the price, time for development, the level of skill of your users, and the features you want to include in your course.

Classifications of Authoring Tools

Web Authoring

An e-learning course can be considered a type of website or web page. Because of this, any tool that can be used to create a website can be used to create an e-learning course—even if the course will not be delivered over the Internet.

Web-authoring tools, such as Adobe Muse, can be a good choice because they are widely used. This means it is easy to find training on how to use the software and easy to find team members who already have the needed skills. You may even have people in your company already (such as in the IT or marketing departments) who know how to use the software.

The disadvantage of web-authoring tools is that they are not designed specifically for e-learning. Therefore, many of the course elements have to be custom built, or you would need to buy third-party software to get around this issue and build some of the course structure for you.

HTML Editors

An HTML editor, such as Adobe Dreamweaver, is a software package that allows you to build HTML pages either by creating the code yourself or by designing the pages visually and allowing the software to create the code behind the scenes.

Courses created with an HTML editor tend to be low bandwidth, easy to update, and very compatible on different operating platforms. In addition, web programmers can use programming languages (such as JavaScript) to create advanced features.

 Caution: Flash-Only Output

If you want your courses to play on an iPhone or iPad, be careful about any tool that only outputs to Flash formats. Look for tools that offer HTML5-friendly output, and be sure to test your courses carefully on those devices before getting too far into your decision-making process.

Media and Application Tools

For more interactivity and media, you could consider using more advanced web applications such as Adobe Flash or After Effects. These programs are designed to create slick visual presentations and are even used to build new software programs. The capabilities are almost endless, but the learning curve is extensive.

Course Authoring

Years ago, programming skills were required to create any sort of computer-based training. However, today, there are more and more tools that are built for the non-techie. Some systems are template or form based and very easy to learn and use. Other systems are more flexible, but only require the use of menus and dialog boxes rather than coding.

These tools, such as Trivantis Lectora, Articulate Studio and Storyline, and Adobe Captivate, are easy to learn and use. They can be used in a rapid development environment (meaning you are looking for quicker turnaround times and using solutions that don't require programming), and especially when you want subject matter experts to help build the content.

The downside of such tools is that you are locked into the features that come with the software and may not get every feature you want.

FIGURE 4-1: ADOBE CAPTIVATE COURSE AUTHORING TOOL

PowerPoint Conversion Tools

Several tools on the market automatically convert PowerPoint presentations into an online course. Many of the software packages listed in the previous sections have the ability to import content from these programs, but there are also tools that allow you to author 100 percent in PowerPoint.

Some of these conversion tools simply convert the PowerPoint document to a Flash file or other web-enabled format. While this doesn't make for very interactive learning, it makes it easy to launch and track the presentation on your LMS.

Other conversion tools let you add e-learning elements such as interactions, quizzing, and tracking, available on a new menu in your PowerPoint software. Two examples are Articulate Studio and AdobePresenter.

These tools allow for the shortest learning curve and development time, as well as for any number of end users to create content. The downsides are that you are limited to the templates and features available and that the final product may really look more like an online presentation than online learning.

FIGURE 4-2: ARTICULATE STUDIO TEMPLATE DESIGN SAMPLE

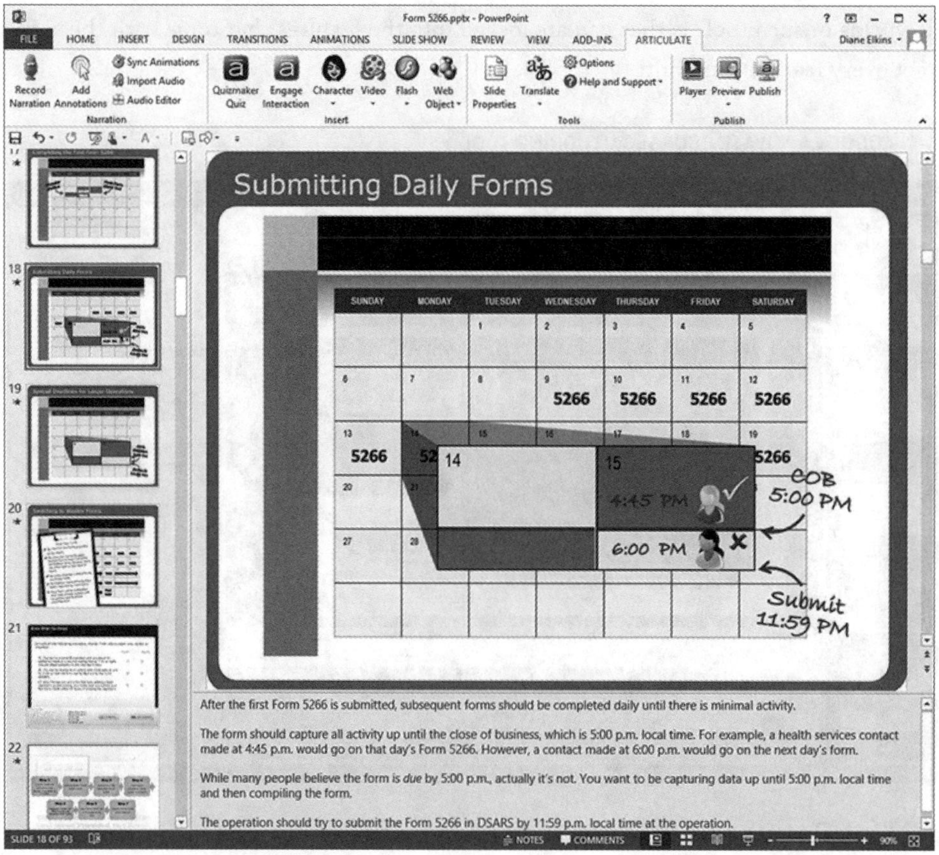

Image provided courtesy of American Red Cross.

The Great Debate: PowerPoint Conversion

Is the quick conversion of PowerPoint slides into e-learning a good thing? The challenge is that these tools make it quicker and easier than ever to create bad e-learning. A PowerPoint that isn't effective in the classroom will be even less effective as e-learning. But bad design isn't the fault of the tool. If e-learning is designed thoughtfully, PowerPoint conversion tools can still be effective.

Features of Authoring Tools

As you gather data to consider what features you want to build into your courses, one constraint on your decision is what your authoring tool can do. Figure 4-3 lists many possible features to be included in an authoring tool. Use it to create your wish list, to help you create an RFP, to compare and rank similar products, or to make design decisions.

 FIGURE 4-3: SAMPLE COURSE-AUTHORING TOOL CHECKLIST

Feature	Importance	Tool 1	Tool 2
General			
Company name			
Website			
Access to demo			
Installed or cloud based			
Purchase price			
Maintenance and upgrade fees			
Other fees			
Training provided			
Support provided			
Can be bought alone (not with LMS)			
Company Information			
Years in business			
Number of users			
Year this tool was released			
Year this version was released			
Media			
Audio			
Accepts audio files (which formats?)			
Plug-ins or players learners need to play audio			

 Jargon Alert:

You'll find each of these terms in the table of features. You'll learn more about these in chapter 6.

- **SCORM/AICC/ Tin Can**—Interoperability standards that ensure e-learning products work together; for example, a SCORM-compliant course should successfully send data to a SCORM-compliant LMS.

- **Section 508**—Federal law for accessibility of electronic communications to people with disabilities; if a course is Section 508 compliant, it meets the guidelines for people with visual, auditory, or motor disabilities.

The entire checklist can be found here: www.td.org/elearningtools

Element Tools

While an authoring tool helps you assemble your course as a whole, you may also need tools to help you with individual course elements. These elements can then be pasted or imported into your authoring tool. In some cases, your authoring tool may have the capability to create these elements and you wouldn't need a separate tool.

Graphics

At a minimum, you will want the ability to crop and resize graphics and change the file type. Many authoring tools have this capability, but some do not. If you are more ambitious, you may want the ability to edit or create graphics yourself.

Photo-Editing Software

In addition to cropping and resizing graphics, you may want the ability to edit or manipulate graphics. For example, in a course on customer conflict, you may want to find a picture of an angry customer and make the whole photo red. Perhaps you would like to create a photo collage for a title graphic. Or maybe you returned from a photo shoot from your manufacturing floor and you need to lighten up some of the pictures.

Photo editing packages such as Adobe Photoshop or Photoshop Elements or Snagit by TechSmith give you the ability to modify and enhance photos and other graphics.

FIGURE 4-4: SNAGIT BY TECHSMITH PHOTO EDITING SCREEN

Graphics-Creation Software

You may want the ability to custom-create graphics. Perhaps you want to create a cartoon character to serve as the "host" of the course. Maybe there are diagrams or processes you need to illustrate, or maybe you want to create your own interface buttons. Here are some choices:

- illustration software, such as Adobe Illustrator

- photo-editing software (some have drawing capability), such as Adobe Photoshop or TechSmith Snagit

- end-user business applications, such as Microsoft PowerPoint

- animation software, such as Adobe Edge Animate.

FIGURE 4-5: GRAPHIC OPTIONS WITH MICROSOFT POWERPOINT

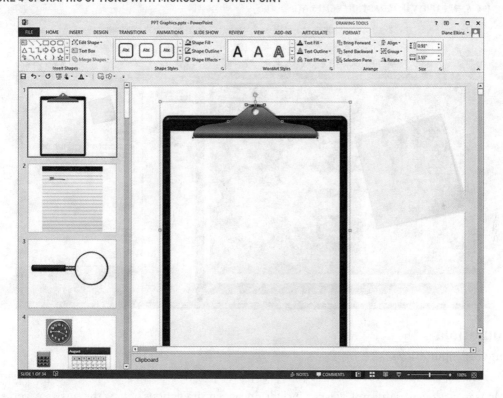

Interactions and Animations

Once again, the authoring tool you use may provide the ability to create the interactions (such as a roll-over screen) and animations (such as a moving diagram of a chemical or manufacturing process) you want. However, the use of animation software often allows you to create more advanced, more flexible, and more creative interactive elements. Adobe Flash has long been the industry standard for creating such custom interactions, but its output is not directly compatible with iPads and iPhones. Adobe Edge Animate is a popular replacement for creating animations (but not interactivity).

Another option is using a template-based interaction software, such as Articulate Engage or Raptivity, which allow you to easily add your content to the template to significantly decrease development time.

FIGURE 4-6: RAPTIVITY INTERACTION TEMPLATE

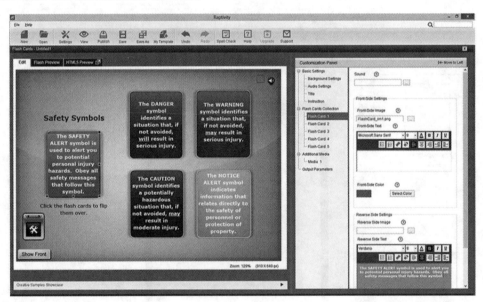

Simulations

Computer Simulations

When creating courses designed to teach software applications (such as an order-processing or customer-relations management software), you can include on-screen simulations of how the software works. You can even create practice or testing sessions where learners may try the steps themselves.

Special tools are available that make it quick and easy to create these simulations. With tools such as Adobe Captivate, TechSmith Camtasia, and Articulate Storyline and Articulate Studio, you can create a short software simulation in a few hours.

FIGURE 4-7: TECHSMITH CAMTASIA SIMULATION SOFTWARE

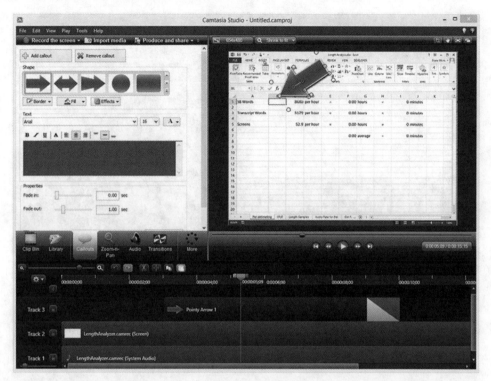

Business and Technical Simulations

One way to make sure your learners know how to apply what they have learned back on the job is to create a real-world simulation. These simulations may just be a series of screens outlining a situation, followed by some multiple-choice questions. This type of simulation or scenario can often be done in your authoring tool.

However, some software packages are available that allow you to create more complex and interactive business simulations where the learners control variables, make decisions, and see the impact of their choices. Tools include Rehearsal VRP (video role-play) and PeopleSIM. Some of these companies have premade simulations you can integrate into your courses.

FIGURE 4-8: REHEARSAL VRP SIMULATION SOFTWARE

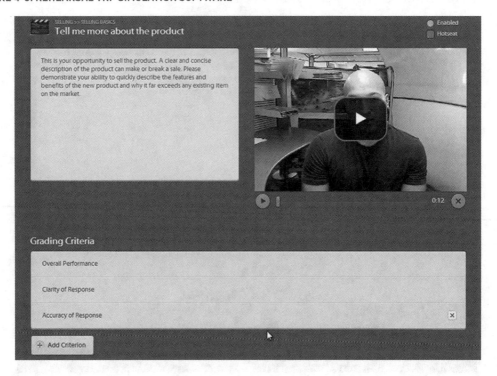

Assessments

Most authoring tools, learning management systems, and learning content management systems have the ability to create tests and assessments. In addition, you may want to look at software specifically designed for that purpose.

Quizzes and Tests

Tools such as Questionmark Perception and Articulate Quizmaker allow you to create and manage tests and exams.

FIGURE 4-9: ARTICULATE QUIZMAKER SAMPLE QUIZ

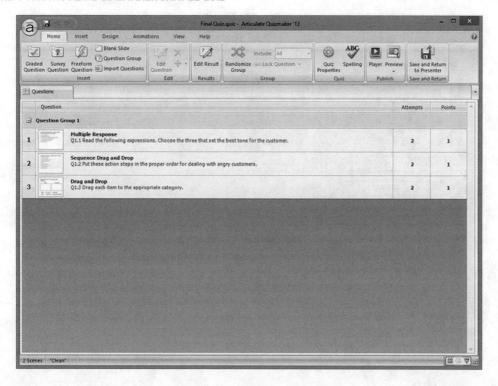

Games

If you'd like to get more creative with your quizzing and assessments, you may want to consider software that lets you create online games. There may be game capabilities in your authoring tool or in regular assessment software, or you can look at tools designed specifically for games, such as BRAVO! (C3 Soft-Works) and Raptivity (Harbinger Group).

FIGURE 4-10: MY BILLIONAIRE GAME FROM BRAVO!

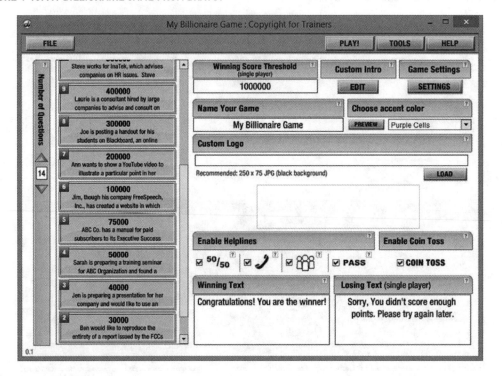

Audio and Video

In many ways, audio and video are a whole world of their own. If you plan to record and edit your own audio and video, you may need to acquire both equipment and software to do what you want to do. At the simplest level, you may be able to record audio clips in your authoring tool or even in PowerPoint. This is a quick and easy way to record, but there are limited editing options. You might need to rerecord whenever there is a change or a mistake.

Many e-learning developers use Audacity for audio editing because it is relatively easy to use . . . and it's free. For video, tools such as Microsoft Windows Movie Maker, Adobe Premiere or Premiere Elements, and Adobe Director provide a nice balance of capability and ease of use.

On the high end, you could purchase very expensive equipment to record, mix, and edit audio and video. However, unless you have a large-scale production effort or other needs in the company for similar services, it is often best to contract out any high-end media production.

📖 **Dive Deeper**

Rapid Video Development for Trainers: How to Create Learning Videos Fast and Affordably by Jonathan Halls

FIGURE 4-11: AUDACITY AUDIO EDITING SOFTWARE

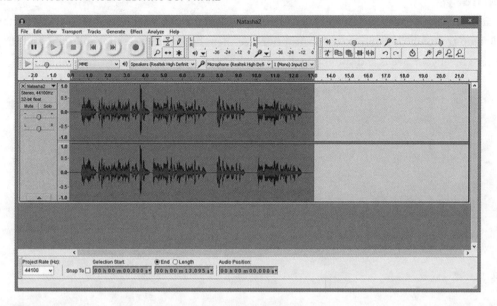

FIGURE 4-12: ADOBE PREMIERE ELEMENTS VIDEO EDITING SOFTWARE

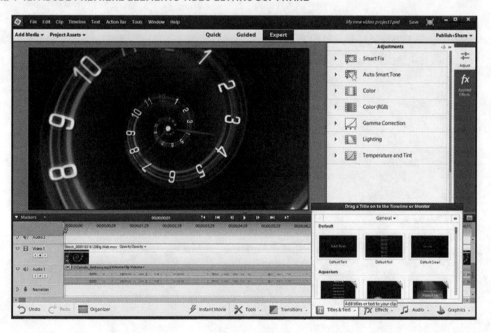

Summary

There are many options that allow you to create, deliver, and manage your e-learning. It is important to establish up front which features you want, prioritize them based on necessity, and then find the best product to meet your needs and your budget.

5

THE ANALYSIS PHASE

Since the ADDIE model (analyze, design, develop, implement, evaluate) is widely used to manage training development, this book is organized to follow this model.

The analysis, or first, phase of the model actually began during your strategy and project planning phases. The analysis continues here as you gather information that helps you make a number of design decisions about your e-learning courses.

The goal of analysis is to ask the right questions and discover information about the business environment, learners, and technology in the organization so you can determine the most effective course design.

 ### The Great Debate: The ADDIE Model

The instructional design community has a love/hate relationship with the ADDIE model. Many feel it is outdated, slow, and rigid, and some have proposed alternate models, such as SAM (successive approximation model). Proponents of ADDIE say it is still a valid method and that many newer models are simply repackaged versions of the same steps that are in ADDIE.

On most training development projects, the phases of the ADDIE model are not distinct and finite, but rather they blend together and overlap. As you get more specific in the analysis phase, it is useful to think about how you will use that information during the design phase. For example, you will ask technology questions during this phase so you can make decisions about e-learning format and media usage in the next phase. Analyzing the audience now will help you make decisions about everything from module length to writing style to testing strategies later.

 ## Dive Deeper

Rapid Instructional Design by George M. Piskurich

The Accidental Instructional Designer by Cammy Bean

Leaving ADDIE for SAM: An Agile Model for Developing the Best Learning Experiences by Michael Allen with Richard Sites

Much of the analysis you will conduct would be the same whether you are looking at traditional classroom training or e-learning. If you are not familiar with the process, there are excellent resources to help you understand your needs and goals.

While this chapter includes elements that could be useful for classroom training analysis, its main focus is the elements that are unique to e-learning.

Business Analysis

Any business training, regardless of the format, should fit a specific business need. Conducting a business analysis will not only help you decide whether you need training and what to train on, but it will also help you uncover issues that would affect how you structure, present, and test on the material.

The Problem

Training professionals are often given a problem that the organization is facing and are told to solve it with training. Since not all problems have training solutions, it is important to thoroughly understand the real problem so you can find the best way to solve it. The questions you must ask to get to the root of the problem are no different for an e-learning program than they are for a classroom program.

You may have to ask multiple questions (for example, why? how?) and look at all levels of the organization to find your answers. Remember, during the analysis phase, you are merely asking the questions and documenting the answers. In the design phase, you make the decisions about how to approach the situation.

FIGURE 5-1: PROBLEM ANALYSIS CHECKLIST

Question	Answer
What is the problem?	
What caused the problem?	
Where is the problem (certain department, entire organization, etc.)?	
When did the problem begin?	
Is the problem persistent?	
Has the problem ever occurred before?	
What are the issues that surround the problem?	
Has anyone tried to fix the problem before? If yes, how did they try to fix it and what was the outcome?	
How was the problem discovered?	
What are the consequences if the problem continues?	
What are the benefits if the problem is solved/lessened?	
Are there legal or compliance issues involved?	

Specifically, asking these questions will help you understand:

- whether training will solve the problem
- when training won't solve the problem, whether it can still help in some way
- who needs the training
- who should be involved in development
- what the objectives should be
- what information to include
- how that information would best be taught
- if e-learning would be a good format.

The Business

Understanding the overall business environment also helps you make decisions about how to approach training—whether classroom or computer based. The answers to some of the questions in the Business Analysis Checklist may be obvious if you are inside the organization, but it is still worth the time to document the answers.

Look at the organization as a whole—at the type of business and how it is laid out—so you can later decide how to get the training to those who need it. You'll see in subsequent chapters that the size and structure of the organization could be a big factor in your choice of a classroom delivery or an e-learning platform.

 Tips From the Pros: An Example—Low Sales

Say you are told that sales have decreased 30 percent during the last quarter and you need to find the cause. You may find the cause is a change in a customer-service policy or perhaps the release of a new product that the sales force doesn't really understand how to present to customers.

If the issue is the policy, that would suggest a review of the policy would help most, rather than training. If the issue is the new product, then maybe some quick training is needed on features, along with discussions on how to present the product. If just product knowledge is needed, self-paced training might be effective. If discussion is necessary to help the sales team determine how to apply the information in real-world situations, perhaps a blended learning solution would work best so that the sales people could discuss different scenarios and options in a classroom setting.

FIGURE 5-2: BUSINESS ANALYSIS CHECKLIST

Question	Answer
What is the business (retail, manufacturing, etc.)?	
What types of tasks do the employees do?	
What are the job classes (manager, associate, etc.)?	
How many locations are there?	
How spread out are the locations? Different countries? Time zones?	
What are the different departments?	
How many employees are there?	
What is the business culture?	
What is the turnover rate for the organization?	
Who are the decision makers in the organization?	
Are there corporate communication guidelines you need to adhere to (fonts, colors, logo usage)?	

Specifically, these questions will help you decide:

- the style and tone of the interface, graphics, and language
- the best format (classroom, e-learning, or type of e-learning)
- the cost-effectiveness of an e-learning solution.

For example, a traditional, conservative financial institution may not be suited for game-based simulations; similarly, an organization with locations throughout the world may not be able to support live webcasts because of time-zone differences.

The Learning Environment

Many of the questions that help you make your training decisions may revolve around the learning culture and environment for the entire organization. (You'll answer questions about the target audience itself in the Audience Analysis Checklist.) Now you'll want to gather information about what learning strategies have been used in the past, what has worked, and what hasn't. You may want to find out what made learning successful in the organization and how different strategies were received.

If e-learning has been used by the organization, find out everything you can about what topics were rolled out, how it was designed, and how the learners responded.

There may also be requirements that have been put in place about learning—guidelines such as who can take training, for how long, and in what format. Be sure to note whether your answers are true for all training, for a specific course, or for a certain group of courses.

FIGURE 5-3: LEARNING ENVIRONMENT ANALYSIS CHECKLIST

Question	Answer
How is training perceived in the organization? - By upper management? - By the target audience? - By the supervisors of the target audience?	
What types of training have been used before?	
What types of training have been successful?	
What learning incentives have been used in the past—positive and negative?	
What disincentives to completing training might exist?	
Are there limitations on who can take classes (for example, by job function, job title, or employment status)?	
Who is in charge of training?	
How much money is in the budget for training?	
Who is most likely to develop the training: training department, contractors, subject matter experts?	
How often will the material change/need to be updated?	
Do you have mandatory training requirements? Self-imposed requirements?	
Do you have mandatory testing requirements? Self-imposed requirements?	
Do you need to prove to anyone that the training was completed? Passed?	

FIGURE 5-3: LEARNING ENVIRONMENT ANALYSIS CHECKLIST (CONTINUED)

Question	Answer
Are grades important?	
In what ways is training tied to performance (such as bonuses, appraisals, etc.)	
How long can the target audience typically get away for when they need training?	
Should a learner pick and choose courses?	
Should a learner pick which sections of a course to take?	
Do the learners need to take the training even if they know the information?	
Has e-learning been introduced to the organization? With what reaction and result?	
What tracking and reporting needs do you have?	
Do you have certain training that must be taken again annually?	

Knowing the answers to these questions can help you decide:

- whether e-learning is a good fit
- how hard you might need to "sell" e-learning to the organization
- whether you need an LMS and with what features
- what kind of navigation and testing to include in the course
- how long to make each course or module
- which authoring tool might be best
- how you will plan your implementation.

For example, in an environment where frontline supervisors are not very supportive of training, it might be challenging for employees to get away from their work long enough to take an online course. You'll want to consider this when creating your implementation plan.

If you have compliance needs, you may want to set up navigation so that learners view every screen of a course whether they know the information or not. In another case, you may allow learners to freely pick and choose what they want to learn, or maybe even test out of the information they already know.

Audience Analysis

The audience analysis is your key to understanding learners' abilities to take your course and learn the material. Analyze everything—from your audience's language abilities and computer knowledge to their motivations and existing knowledge on the subjects being taught.

Some additional questions you'll want to ask may be decided based on the answers to your business analysis, so remain flexible during this process. For example, you may want to look at the overall demographics for an entire company, but in a global company, you may also want to find information for each individual location. You may find that one branch has something unique that requires special thought in the design phase.

FIGURE 5-4: AUDIENCE ANALYSIS CHECKLIST

Question	Answer
Demographics	
What are the different age groups?	
What are their educational backgrounds?	
What is their English proficiency (reading, writing, listening)?	
What other languages are spoken that might be preferable for the training?	
Are there literacy issues?	
What is the reading level of the group?	
Work Environment	
Will learners be taking courses from home?	
Will learners be taking courses while traveling?	
Does the environment have interruptions?	
Does the environment have noise?	
Will noise disrupt the learners' environment?	
What shift(s) do they have?	
When will they take the training?	

FIGURE 5-4: AUDIENCE ANALYSIS CHECKLIST (CONTINUED)

Question	Answer
Computer Knowledge	
Are learners comfortable using computers? - What is their computer proficiency? - What are the different proficiencies within the target audience?	
Are learners comfortable with the e-learning format?	
Subject Matter	
What level of knowledge do learners already have?	
What experiences have they had with subject?	
Are they likely to need to refer to the material again after training is complete?	
Are they likely to have trouble understanding the information?	
Are they likely to have trouble applying the information?	
Motivation	
How receptive are the learners to training in general?	
How receptive are the learners to THIS topic?	
Are they being forced to go to training?	
Have you had situations where the learners tried to "get around" completing mandatory training?	
Are there concerns about cheating?	
Disabilities and Special Needs	
Is there anyone in the target audience with special auditory needs?	
Is there anyone in the target audience with special visual needs?	
Is there anyone in the target audience with special motor skills needs?	
Is there anyone in the target audience with special cognitive needs?	

Knowing more about your audience can help you make decisions about:

- what format to use for the training

- whether to use fixed versus flexible navigation

- how to structure testing

- whether to make the course Section 508 compliant or perhaps use some of the programming guidelines found in that requirement

- how to present your information (style, graphics, benefits, language)

- what advanced course features to use or leave out

- what help features and instructions to use

- where the training should take place

- what information to include, leave out, or allow people to test out of.

For example, if there are possible issues with learner motivation or a history of sharing answers on a test, you may want to build in a secure password system and a randomized test bank to strengthen the integrity of the test records. If the topic is likely to be met with resistance, perhaps combining a self-paced course with a classroom session or webcast would be best so that the instructor can gauge and respond to that resistance.

Technology Analysis

Analyzing your technology is unique to e-learning, compared to classroom training. For this part of the analysis process, focus on what technology your organization has in place that could support or hinder e-learning.

This analysis can be harder than it looks. It is often easy to find the "norm" for the company, but there may be a few computers, workstations, or just one person who works from home who could extend your search for information.

During the technology analysis, you want to find the worst case for each question. For example, the computers may all have sound cards, but 10 percent don't have speakers. While that doesn't mean you need to design for the 10 percent, you need to know this to decide if audio is a viable option.

Work closely with your IT department, if you have one, so you can make sure you haven't missed anything.

FIGURE 5-5: TECHNOLOGY ANALYSIS CHECKLIST

Question	Answer
Technology for Learner Computers	
Do they have speakers or headphones?	
Do they have a sound card?	
What is the processor speed?	
What operating system are they using?	
Do they have Internet access?	
What is the browser type and version?	
What is the connection speed?	
What is the screen size?	
How much memory do they have?	
Do they have a webcam?	
Do they have video playback capability?	
What drives are available (CD, USB, DVD)?	
Is a printer available?	
Do they have a microphone?	
What version of the Flash player is installed?	
Mobile	
Will they be using mobile devices?	
Which devices?	
Which operating systems?	
Which versions of which browsers?	

FIGURE 5-5: TECHNOLOGY ANALYSIS CHECKLIST (CONTINUED)

Question	Answer
Restrictions	
What is their bandwidth?	
Is there a firewall?	
Can they download and install files?	
Are there guidelines for individual file sizes?	
Are there certain websites that are blocked?	
Miscellaneous	
Will anyone be accessing the courses through a remote network (such as Citrix)?	
Would any information need to move between your course and other systems?	
Would your courses need to be SCORM, AICC, or SCORM compliant?	

Understanding this information will help you make decisions about:

- what authoring tool to use
- whether you need to set up dedicated training stations
- what file size, plug-in, and other design restrictions you might have
- what type of media can be used
- what upgrades might be necessary for implementation.

For example, if learners are not allowed to download and install files on their computers, some courses will not work. Some off-the-shelf courseware requires files to be loaded temporarily to the computer before they are played.

Summary

During the analysis phase you want to gather valuable information that will help you make decisions about your training. Ask questions about the problem, business, audience, and technology. Once you have the answers to your questions, use the design phase to decide what solutions are best and what your objectives will be. The next three chapters explain what to do with the information you have gathered and how to make design decisions that you will use when developing your course.

6

THE DESIGN PHASE: BROAD STRATEGIES

During the analysis phase, you asked a lot of people a lot of questions and documented a lot of answers. Now it's time to turn those answers into a new question: What does this mean for the training? Where the analysis phase was about gathering information, the design phase is about making decisions based on that information.

Many of the decisions are the same, regardless of whether you are looking at classroom training or e-learning; however, some are unique to e-learning. While this chapter addresses overall strategies, chapters 7 and 8 examine specific design decisions about course features and functions.

E-Learning and Instructional Design

Within the ADDIE model, the design phase helps you make decisions about whether or not you need training, what you need to teach, and the best way to teach it. You will create a road map of what you want to accomplish and how you plan to get there. If the design phase is conducted and documented properly, any training developer could pick up this road map and begin to develop the training.

There are many interpretations of what steps should be included in the design phase. These steps are some of the most common:

- develop learning objectives
- determine prerequisite skills
- create a content outline
- decide on instructional strategies for content presentation, practice activities, and assessments
- choose the right delivery system
- create test questions
- decide on course features, functions, and design
- create a design document.

If you have never developed training before or have never had formal instruction in the training design or development process, you may want to do some research on your own. While this book addresses many instructional design issues, it is not intended to be an instructional design text. Instead, the goal is to give you a basic understanding of all the tasks you will need to perform, and a deeper understanding of what is unique to the development of an e-learning project.

For example, this book shows you how the steps to developing objectives relate to e-learning, but not everything you would need to know to create them.

 Dive Deeper: Instructional Design Resources

The Accidental Instructional Designer by Cammy Bean.
Rapid Instructional Design by George Piskurich
ISD From the Ground Up by Chuck Hodell
Training Design Basics by Saul Carliner
The Mager Six-Pack by Robert F. Mager
- *Analyzing Performance Problems* (with Peter Pipe)
- *Preparing Instructional Objectives*
- *Measuring Instructional Results*
- *How to Turn Learners On . . . Without Turning Them Off*
- *Goal Analysis*
- *Making Instruction Work*

Developing Objectives

"Do we have to know this?"

"Is this going to be on the test?!?!"

At a very early age, we understood the concept of a learning objective. Unfortunately, training is sometimes designed and developed without taking the time to formally identify what the learner is supposed to get out of the training. This can result in frustrated learners (who don't know what they are supposed to be learning), inefficient training (that includes more than is necessary), or worse, ineffective training (that doesn't accomplish its goal).

Deciding on Your Objectives

During the analysis phase, you identified business problems or opportunities, identified underlying causes, and looked at potential solutions. It's now time to separate out the solutions you will implement that involve training and break them down into specific learning objectives. According to the *ASTD Handbook*, learning objectives are "clear, measurable statements of behavior that a learner must demonstrate for training to be considered a success."

Objectives help you decide what to include in the course, help the learners understand what they will get and what will be expected of them, and help you evaluate the learner and the course.

You may even want to create a hierarchy of objectives. For example, you may have course objectives, module objectives, and section objectives.

Prerequisites

In addition to determining what the objectives should be, you also want to determine what they should not be. For a number of reasons, you will want to take the time to identify the knowledge, skills, and abilities you expect the learners to have before taking the course. This helps you:

- decide what not to include in the course
- notify the learner up front of the expectations
- set up prerequisite training requirements, especially if you have a learning management system that can track such things
- develop your content to the right level of knowledge.

How Should They Be Phrased?

Elements

A strong learning objective covers only one point, is focused on what the learner will do, and generally contains a behavioral outcome, a condition, and a success criterion or standard.

For example: "Given a computer simulation, you will be able to use the XYZ scheduling software to create a schedule for all assembly-line workers that satisfies estimated production volume, requires no overtime, and complies with all labor and union laws."

Testability

A good learning objective is one that allows the learner's mastery of it to be tested. In the world of e-learning, the relationship between objectives and testing might cause you to reevaluate your objectives, especially if you are converting classroom training to e-learning. This is because your test options may be limited in an e-learning environment.

For example, you may have a classroom training objective that states: "Upon completion of this module, you will be able to discuss the differences between a learning management system and a learning content management system." If the class is conducted via self-paced e-learning without an instructor, will they have the ability to truly discuss the difference? If your question options are limited to multiple-choice questions, perhaps the best you can do is see if they can recognize the difference between an LMS and an LCMS. So then you have to make a decision: Do you revise the objective or do you rethink your training format and testing options?

Other examples of objective verbs that are difficult to evaluate in a self-paced course include:

- define (perhaps to be replaced with *recognize the definition of*)
- list (replaced with *select from a list*)
- explain (replaced with *identify*).

Using scenarios and simulations may help you with more advanced objective types. For example, you may have an objective that asks your learners to demonstrate a procedure or assemble a piece of equipment. If you can include an accurate online simulation, you may be able to keep those objectives, but stipulate that a simulation will be used.

Structuring the Content

Once you have your objectives defined, you can begin to organize your content. During this part of the process, you will decide on the order and flow of the material. For example, you may want to organize the information in the order that it will come up on the job (such as a series of business, computer, or manufacturing processes), from the simple to the complex (such as scientific information or business theories), or from the general to the specific (such as employee orientation information about the industry, the company, then the department).

Content Sequence and Flow

To help you with sequencing, you may want to create a flow chart, as shown in Figure 6-1, to help you and your developers visualize the big picture.

FIGURE 6-1: SAMPLE SEQUENCING FLOW CHART

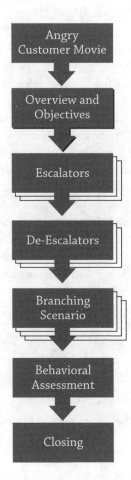

Course Hierarchy and Outline

With an e-learning course especially, you'll want to decide how the course can be broken down into chunks.

First, you'll consider the question conceptually. You can determine how many levels in the course there will be. For example, will you have a course made of modules, with each module containing lessons? You might also want guidelines about when to break something into its own module or lesson. You may even want to outline how much information should go on a single screen.

From there, you'll want to map out the actual content points to be included, in outline form. You are not writing the content at this stage, but you are outlining the courses, modules, and lessons.

The Great Debate: Formal Objectives

Do you include your formal objectives in your e-learning course? There are several schools of thought.

- **Don't include them.** Some people feel the objectives are used only for the training developers and do not need to be presented to the learner. Instead of formal objectives, you may want to use more benefits-driven marketing language to both sell and explain what is covered.
- **Put them at the beginning of the course.** The complete list of objectives may appear on one of the screens in the overview or introduction of the course.
- **Put them near the beginning of the course.** Because a formal objectives slide can be somewhat dry, consider telling a story to build interest in the course first, and then follow that with a screen of objectives. This is like TV shows getting the viewer's interest when the show starts and showing the credits after the first commercial break.
- **Put them in the course catalog.** Depending upon how you are hosting your courses, it may be best for the learners to be able to see the objectives in the course catalog or launch page so that they can decide if the course will meet their needs before committing to taking it.

You may even choose to outline the individual screens at this point or leave that up to the developer. (Having a content list or outline for each screen will help your developers stay focused and succinct. Wordy or wandering e-learning gets expensive, so you'll want to make sure everyone knows exactly what they need to say—and don't need to say.)

Be sure to double-check that your outline contains enough information to meet the learning objectives and doesn't contain information that is not needed to meet them.

Instructional Strategies

For each objective, determine the best way to present the information, to allow for practice and feedback, and to assess the learner's performance.

Decisions about instructional strategies generally drive the format you select for training (for example, classroom or on the job), and, if e-learning is chosen, drive the selection of your authoring tool. However, in some cases, the format and even authoring tool may be selected (or dictated) in advance, in which case the tool may drive the instructional strategies.

For example, you could pick a tool because you know you want a randomized bank of questions. (Select the tool based on instructional strategy.) Or you might need to specify only multiple-choice and true/false questions because that is all your tool can support. (Select instructional strategy based on the tool.)

Ideally, you would decide what the best way to train is and then find the platform and tool to support that. Technology should support training decisions, not drive them. However, sometimes the reality of the situation wins out. You may already be locked into a certain tool or perhaps can't afford to buy or learn a tool that gives you all the options and features you really want. In these cases, you must weigh the benefits and the drawbacks and make the best decision that fits the training need and the business environment.

Presentation

Now that you have your objectives, you will need to decide the best way to present that information to the learner. That decision can be made based on a number of factors such as:

- **Type of information**—Is it a fact, concept, attitude, procedure, behavior? Is it simple or complex? Is it likely to cause resistance or confusion?

- **What you want them to do with the information**—Do you want them to know something, believe something, or do something?

- **The level of mastery you want them to have**—Do you want them to be able to recall, comprehend, or apply a fact or concept? For a skill or procedure, do you want them to be able to perform it on their own or with guidance?

There are numerous possible presentation strategies:

- video presentation (live or recorded)

- audio presentation (live or recorded)

- text narrative

- lecture

- question and answer

- reflection

- on-the-job training

- mentoring or coaching

- scenarios

- simulations

- diagrams

> 📖 **Dive Deeper**
>
> Refer to Benjamin Bloom's taxonomies for educational objectives for more information on these areas: the Cognitive (mental processes), Affective (attitudes, beliefs, and values), and Psychomotor (physical movement and coordination) domains.

- exploratory activities
- demonstrations
- discussions
- group activities
- self-directed research
- documents to be read
- assignments.

As you can imagine, some of these strategies would lend themselves well to self-paced e-learning, some to synchronous learning, and some to classroom training. By selecting the best instructional strategies for each objective, you'll begin to create a picture of how your courses should be designed.

Practice

Effective training gives the learners an opportunity to practice and receive feedback. For each objective in your course, you want to determine the best way to provide that practice and feedback.

Here are some common practice options:

- fact checks (simple questions sprinkled throughout the presentation)
- simulated role plays
- games
- scenario situations
- branching simulations
- simulated practices
- hands-on practices
- group projects
- written exercises.

Think about how feedback can be provided—especially in a self-paced course. Could you provide standard feedback to everyone programmatically? Could you provide individual feedback programmatically? Would you need a person to review the learner's work? Would you need a person to observe the learner?

In addition, you'll want to decide what types of assistance or hints you might provide. For example, would the learners have the benefit of a book or job aid? Could they try the practice activity more than once? Could you provide hints or links back to where the content was originally taught?

Assessment

When making decisions about testing or assessments, you'll consider many of the same issues as with reinforcing practice and can use the same list of strategies. But with a formal assessment, you'll want to consider a few other factors as well:

- Do you want a pretest and post-test?
- Do you want unit assessments, module assessments, or course assessments?
- Will you want to put security procedures in place to increase the integrity of the results?
- Do you want the learners to have more than one try or receive assistance?
- Can the learners refer to any materials or work together?
- Can the learners view the final score, the result of each question, the correct answer to each question, or the reason behind the correct answer? Can they see this after each question or at the end of the test?

Outlining the Instructional Strategies

Once you have made your decisions, outline this information in a design document or lesson plan. You can use a simple table, as in Figure 6-2, to capture your decisions or options for each objective.

FIGURE 6-2: LESSON PLAN GRID

Objective	Type of Information	Presentation	Practice	Assessment
Set up an out-of-office message in Outlook	Procedure	Demonstration (live or simulated) with narrative text (written or presented) to provide context	Hands-on practice, either simulated or in a live system, with the ability to reference the procedure if needed, and feedback for each step (either system generated or provided by an instructor)	Hands-on practice in a real or simulated environment without reference to the procedure. Correct or incorrect feedback provided, but without explanation or assistance

Selecting the Best Format

You may feel as if you chose e-learning all the way back in chapter 1 when you first reviewed the advantages and disadvantages. But this book's approach asks that you hold off on your decision until this point. Using a more formal method helps you ensure that the technology is supporting the training, and not vice versa.

As you review your list of instructional strategies, make some determinations about what the best format would be.

Classroom or Distance? Instructor or Self-Paced?

Based on everything you have already decided, it should now be clear whether certain objectives can best be met in a classroom or if the learners can meet them on their own. Even if the latter is true, you'll have a good idea whether an instructor would need to be involved at all or if your course can truly be a stand-alone, self-paced course. When making this decision, look not only at your instructional strategies, but also at your business environment, including factors such as budget, schedule, and volume. You may find that one format is better for instructional design reasons but another format is better for business reasons.

Blended Learning: The Best of Both Worlds

You may find that each format has some value based on the business situation. For example:

- An e-learning format is great for presenting the factual information on a new product being released by your company, but not as good for more subjective elements, such as what objections might be presented by customers and how to handle them.
- Through online video and electronic support documents, you can provide background information and demonstration techniques for a mechanical procedure, but that won't allow the learners to use actual equipment for practice and assessment.

In these situations, you may want a blended approach and use both e-learning and a more traditional format, such as classroom or on-the-job training. The e-learning portion could be completed as prework, and then the classroom used for discussion, application, practice, and assessment.

Special E-Learning Considerations: Standards and Compliance

The design phase is the perfect time to decide if you want or need your courses or other e-learning systems to comply with any industry standards and guidelines.

SCORM, AICC Compliance, and Experience API

If you want your course to talk to your LMS, make sure they are talking the same language. The e-learning industry has three main interoperability standards you can use to make sure the course and LMS talk to each other. One isn't necessarily better than the other; what matters is that the course and LMS use the same one.

SCORM

The Shareable Course Object Reference Model was developed by Rustici Software for the ADL (Advanced Distributed Learning) to help standardize training across the U.S. Department of Defense. When you have a SCORM-compliant LMS and SCORM-compliant courseware, you can have a greater level of confidence that the two will "speak" to each other. There are two SCORM standards: 1.2 and 2004. (Think of the two SCORM versions as speaking Canadian French versus European French.)

AICC

AICC is a similar industry standard designed to increase interoperability between systems. It stands for Aviation Industry CBT Committee and was one of the early e-learning standards. While it is not as common as SCORM, it is still a reliable standard, and there are many authoring tools and LMSs that are AICC compliant.

Experience API

Also called Tin Can API or xAPI, this is the new generation of SCORM. In addition to standard course tracking, this standard allows for more detailed reporting (such as an individual experience in a course), tracking of learning experiences outside of a course (such as reading or commenting on a blog), and tracking experiences outside of a browser (such as in an app).

Section 508 Compliance

Section 508 is a part of the Rehabilitation Act of 1973 as amended in 1998. It provides guidelines for all federal government agencies to ensure their electronic communication is accessible to those with disabilities. E-learning falls under the category of electronic communication.

You may want your courses to be Section 508 compliant for one of two reasons:

- You are a federal government agency or are creating courses for a federal government agency and therefore must be Section 508 compliant.

- You are not required to comply but you know you have people with disabilities in your target audience and you want to use the Section 508 provisions as a guideline to make sure your courses are accessible.

The guidelines ensure compatibility with assistive devices for people with visual, auditory, or motor-skills challenges. Assistive devices include equipment such as a screen reader for someone who can't see the screen and mouse alternatives such as a breathing device that controls the on-screen pointer for someone who cannot use a mouse.

The guidelines also ensure that the course is not reliant on elements that cannot be used by everyone. For example, if there is audio in a course, you want to make sure there is a text alternative for those with hearing disabilities. You would want keyboard alternatives for any action requiring the mouse for those with motor-skills issues that prevent them from using a mouse, or for someone with visual restrictions who cannot see what the mouse needs to do on screen.

 Dive Deeper

For more information about Section 508 compliance, go to www.section508.gov and www.access-board.gov.

Even if you do not need or choose to make your courses Section 508 compliant, consider those in your target audience with disabilities and how they might experience the course. Decide on a strategy to ensure that everyone gets equal access to the training opportunities.

Summary

You now know what needs to be taught (your objectives, that is), the overall structure of the course, some high-level strategies for presentation, practice, and assessment, and some ideas about the best format to use. As you continue through the design phase, you will add even more detail to this plan. Chapters 7 and 8 describe how to translate your instructional plan into specific course features and functions.

7

THE DESIGN PHASE: TESTING AND INTERACTIVITY

By this point in the process, you have identified your audience, their environment, what you need to teach them, and some broad instructional strategies to get you there. Now it is time to translate that information into the specific elements to be used in your courses.

During this part of the design phase, you will make and document decisions about how to handle everything from questions and interactions (chapter 7) to interface design and use of media (chapter 8). These decisions will be collected in your design document and used by the people actually developing the courses.

Testing and Assessments

One of the most commonly cited advantages of moving to an e-learning platform is the ability to provide tests, practice, and feedback. With all the benefits of online testing come a number of different design choices. When making design decisions and constructing your questions, you must first understand your goals, then create a strategy, and, finally, build and evaluate the questions.

Determining Your Testing Goals

There are many variables that go into the design and development of questions in an e-learning course. But before you make these decisions, it is important to first understand why you want to include testing. Once your goals are clear, the decisions become easier.

Use this list as a guide to help you identify your reasons for including testing. (Note that "because I can" is not one of the options!) For any given course, more than one of these reasons may apply:

- **interaction**—to keep learners engaged and involved
- **self-awareness**—to let learners know, for their own benefit, how they are doing; this can help them decide for themselves if they need to go back and restudy any of the information
- **remediation and correction**—to provide learners feedback on their mastery of the material and redirect them as needed
- **reinforcement**—to make sure a certain teaching point is not only learned but also remembered, to reinforce information
- **course direction**—to create customized learning paths for each learner based on what he or she already knows
- **course evaluation**—to determine if the course truly taught what it was supposed to teach
- **learner evaluation**—to assess if the learner knows what you want him or her to know
- **certification**—to be 100 percent sure the learner knows what you want him or her to know and to be able to document it.

Creating a Testing Strategy

Once you understand the goals of your testing, you can move forward with creating a testing strategy. This includes a number of one-time decisions about how questions will be structured, written, programmed, and presented.

Question Types

The types of questions you use would ideally be driven by the type of content you have and the specific objectives. However, sometimes your question types may be dictated by the authoring tool you are using or by whether or not you have an instructor available. Remember also that you can use a blended strategy for testing: The learner learns the information through e-learning but then is tested in a classroom or work setting by a peer, supervisor, or instructor.

Multiple Choice

Multiple-choice questions are by far the most common in e-learning, whether it is the most appropriate format or not. These question types are best for facts, concepts, and even applications—if developed in a scenario format.

FIGURE 7-1: EXAMPLE OF A MULTIPLE-CHOICE QUESTION

Which of the following actions is a DE-escalator?

○ Explaining why the situation isn't your fault.

○ Explaining what the customer should have done differently.

◉ Explaining what you are doing.

○ Explaining what you are not able to do and why.

Here are some design and programming decisions you'll need to make about multiple-choice questions:

- Will there be only one right answer or multiple right answers?

- How many options can you have? Do the options have to be the same for every question?

- How will the options be presented? Check boxes, radio buttons, drop-down menu, or hot spot?

When developing multiple-choice questions, keep these tips in mind:

- Use realistic distracters (the "wrong" answers).

- If you are using randomized options, do not put letters next to the options or in the remediation. When appropriate, use "all of these" or "none of these" instead of "all of the above" or "none of the above," so options can be put anywhere on the screen.

- If you are using the word "not" in the question, emphasize it with bolding, capitalization, or underlining, so the learner doesn't accidentally skim over it. For example: Which of the following situations is NOT an example of . . ."

- If learners can pick more than one correct answer, be sure to tell them.

True/False

Many designers do not like true/false questions because they are too easy to guess. Developers often like them because they are easy to write. True/false questions should be saved for straightforward factual information with little room for interpretation, such as policies and procedures.

FIGURE 7-2: EXAMPLE OF A TRUE/FALSE QUESTION

If a customer is raising his voice, it is best to match his tone and volume.

○ True

◉ False

When developing true/false questions, keep these tips in mind:

- Avoid using negative statements; for example: "Decide if the following statement is true or false. New York City is not the capital of the state of New York." Even if the learner knows the negative statement is true, he or she might be confused and select false.

- Be careful not to accidentally put a question mark at the end of the statement being evaluated.

Matching

Matching questions can be programmed many ways in an e-learning course, but all have the learner pair up two different facts, concepts, or even pictures. These questions work well with terminology, classifications, or software commands.

FIGURE 7-3: EXAMPLE OF A MATCHING QUESTION

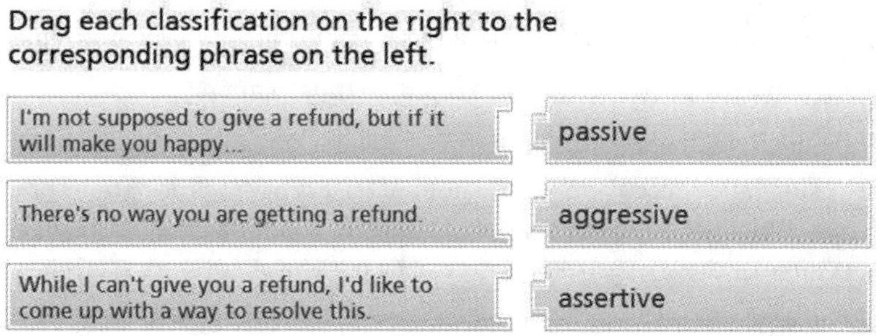

Drag each classification on the right to the corresponding phrase on the left.

I'm not supposed to give a refund, but if it will make you happy...	passive
There's no way you are getting a refund.	aggressive
While I can't give you a refund, I'd like to come up with a way to resolve this.	assertive

There are several design or programming decisions related to matching questions:

- Can you use an option more than once?
- Can you have an option that is not used at all?
- Can you include graphics for half of each pair?
- How will the question function? Click on an option and then its match, type in a letter, drag an imaginary line, or drag an image?

When developing matching questions, keep these tips in mind:

- Be sure to include clear directions about how to operate the question.
- Most learners will assume there is a one-to-one match between the options, so if an option can be used more than once or if there will be an option left over, be sure to point that out.

Fill in the Blank

A fill-in-the-blank question requires a higher level of mastery from the learners because they need to remember the answer on their own, rather than just recognize it in a list. In a truly self-paced environment, grading can be challenging if there are different ways to spell or format the answer.

FIGURE 7-4: EXAMPLE OF A FILL-IN-THE-BLANK QUESTION

My job is to receive complaints about type your text here .

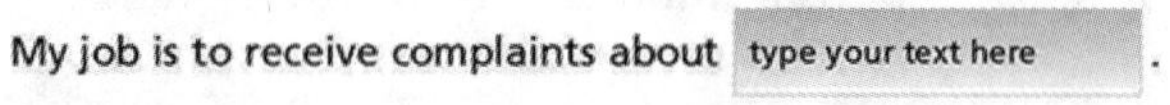

For example, could the correct answer take the singular or plural form? Are there different spellings of the word (such as color and colour)? If the correct answer is a time or date, might some learners format the answer differently than others (especially if they are from different parts of the world)?

Design or programming decisions you'll need to make about fill-in-the-blank questions include:

- Can more than one answer be considered correct? How many maximum?
- Can you have more than one blank per question?

When developing fill-in-the-blank questions, keep these tips in mind:

- Make all blanks equal in length so there's no clue to the answer.
- Brainstorm all the possible answers and different ways to spell, format, or phrase the answer. If there are too many options, consider a different question type.
- Consider whether you want to accept the correct answer even if it is spelled incorrectly. (Are you judging whether they know the answer, whether they can spell the answer, or both?)
- Decide if you want the answer to be case sensitive.

Short Answer and Essay

Short answer and essay questions require a subjective evaluation. In some cases, you can have the answers sent to your LMS or emailed to an instructor for evaluation.

FIGURE 7-5: EXAMPLE OF A SHORT-ANSWER OR ESSAY QUESTION

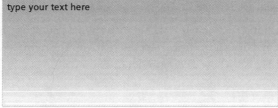

What bad habits do you need to overcome if you are having a bad day at work?

type your text here

Or, you can provide some guidelines to help the students evaluate their own answers. In this case, you can't really grade and track the question. But remember that some of your questions are for the benefit of the student and don't need to be scored and tracked.

Drag and Drop

With a drag-and-drop question, you ask the learner to use the mouse to move some element to a certain part of the screen. There are many variations this question type can take, including labeling parts of a diagram, putting steps in order, or putting information into categories.

FIGURE 7-6: EXAMPLE OF A DRAG-AND-DROP QUESTION

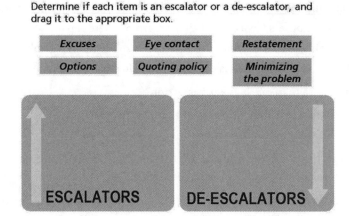

Consider these design decisions regarding drag-and-drop questions:

- If learners make an incorrect choice, will the object still snap into place until they are done with the question, or will it float back to its original spot, letting learners know they need to try again?
- Will there be items that are not used in the answer?

When developing matching questions, keep these tips in mind:

- Try to make the drop spots bigger than the item being dragged. This makes sure you are testing the learners' knowledge and not their mouse skills.

- Make sure the graphics and the technology don't overwhelm the learners. The question should be easy to read and easy to use.

- Provide very clear instructions. If working with a novice audience, just asking them to drag an item on the left and drop it in the correct sequence on the right may not be adequate—you'll probably want to explain how to drag and how to drop.

Simulation

The word *simulation* is defined differently by different people in the world of e-learning. For this discussion, simulation means a simulated environment for a process, software usage, or equipment usage. For example, in a course on math, you may be asked to perform calculations on a simulated on-screen calculator. In a retail course, you may be asked to ring-up a sale on a simulated cash register. In a course on desktop software, you may be given a simulated environment of the software and be asked to perform a procedure.

Because such simulations are job oriented and performance focused, they can be very effective. They are also more expensive to create and maintain.

There are also business simulations, which can often be considered an advanced form of a multiple-choice question. For example, you may have a role-play scenario about how to handle a conflict situation. Different characters are presented and you are asked what you would say in the given situation, selecting your answer from a range of choices provided.

Quiz Games

There are many programs available that allow you to create game-like quizzes. Many of these games operate like popular game shows or board games. They can be a good choice if you need lots of repetition and drilling to make sure your audience truly remembers the information. Games can also be a nice touch when you expect your audience has low motivation for the subject or a low attention span.

When developing questions for games, keep these tips in mind:

- Make sure your instructions are clear. Be careful assuming your learners are familiar with a well-known board game or game-show format—especially if you have a global audience.

- Avoid games when creating a formal assessment or certification. When you want to rely 100 percent on the results of a test, keep it simple.

- Make sure the information lends itself to a game format. Don't let the "coolness" of the game overpower what you are trying to accomplish.

- Avoid games when your audience tends to be straightforward, self-motivated, and has limited time available. This group may find the games distracting or consider them a waste of time.

Gamification

Quiz games are one form of gamification. According to a recent ATD research report:

> Gamification is the integration of game characteristics and mechanics into a real-world training program or task to promote change in behavior. Gamification is most often used to motivate and engage people. Gamification elements may include achievements, badges, levels, rewards, points, and leaderboards. (ATD Research 2014)

Gamification means adding gamelike elements, such as a story, challenge, failure, and rewards. In addition to (or instead of) a quiz set up as a game at the end of the course, the whole course could be presented as a game. For example, as learners complete challenges (which are usually assessment questions), they could earn points, badges, or anything else that would help them accomplish the goal of the game.

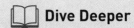

Dive Deeper

The Gamification of Learning and Instruction: Game-Based Methods and Strategies for Training and Education by Karl M. Kapp

Placement

Based on your testing goals, you may want pretests, post-tests, or individual questions embedded throughout the content.

- **Pretests**—Generally, pretests are used in two situations: when you want to judge the effectiveness of the course (comparing "before" knowledge to "after" knowledge) or when you want a custom learning path for the learner. There are several options for using a pretest for custom learning paths:

    o Test results automatically pull up only the content the learner has not mastered, with credit given for the rest of the material.

    o Test results give credit for the material mastered and suggest a path, but the learner can take the entire course, if desired.

    o Test results provide a suggestion for learners to use as they see fit. There is no credit given and all content is available.

- **Post-tests**—These can be included at the end of each lesson, module, course, or even some combination of these. Generally, these tests are scored and tracked. Based on your testing goals, you'll want to decide when the tests are given and how they'll be scored. For example, you may want a post-test at the end of each lesson for reinforcement and to help the learners decide if they are ready to move on. Then you may include a scored and tracked post-test at the end of the entire course that you use for certification purposes.

    You'll also want to decide if you want the test to reside within the course or outside of the course. In some LMS systems, the test is considered a separate learning event. In some cases, the test is built in the LMS instead of in the authoring tool. Often this approach offers more detailed test analysis.

- **Embedded questions**—Most courses have questions sprinkled throughout the content, perhaps every five to seven screens. Generally, these questions are for practice, reinforcement, remediation, and keeping the learner engaged. They are usually not tracked and are most often included just for the benefit of the learner.

- **Number of questions**—Some people choose to specify how many questions will be delivered per learning objective. For example, you may say you want two questions per objective in both the pretest and the post-test. Others instead prefer to let the objective dictate the number of questions needed, as not all objectives are created equal. You will also want to decide if you would use the same questions in the pretest and post-test, or if you would create separate versions of the questions.

Remediation

The term *remediation* can be used broadly to describe any feedback given to a learner during a practice or test exercise. Technically, it means correcting a fault. Based on your testing goals, there are a number of ways to handle remediation and other learner guidance for test and quiz questions. Several options are listed, from least remediation to most remediation.

End-of-Test Remediation

Remediation can be provided as each question is answered or in a summary report given at the end of the test. In general, remediation is saved for the end in very formal assessments and certifications.

- **Final score only**—When you need an extremely reliable test, you may choose to show learners only the final score at the end. This keeps them from simply writing down the answers so they can retake the quiz. It also minimizes sharing of answers. However, it does not provide any real feedback or guidance to learners.

- **Right and wrong indication**—The next level would be to show the final score at the end and let the learners know which questions they did or didn't get right—but without showing them the answers. This again keeps the integrity of your test high and at least lets the learners know what areas they missed.

- **Answers provided for questions missed**—When you want to provide learners with some level of feedback, you may choose to display only the questions they got wrong, along with the correct answer. This increases the remediation for the learner, but does allow them to copy down or share that information. Another downside is that they don't receive confirmation of the correct answer if they merely guessed and got it right.

- **Answers provided for all questions at the end of the test**—Providing answers to all of the questions gives useful direction to learners for areas needing improvement and reinforcement for those questions answered correctly. However, such a summary list would be easy to use when retaking the test or to share with other learners.

Per-Question Remediation

When you want learners to learn from each question as well as be assessed by it, you may choose to provide remediation when each question is answered. Your options may be limited by your authoring tool.

- **Standard for the whole course**—Some systems will allow you to provide remediation for each question, but there can only be one "correct" message and one "incorrect" message for the entire course. This lets learners know if they got the answer right or wrong.

- **Question-specific remediation without explanation**—This indicates whether or not learners got the answer right and what the right answer is but with no explanation as to why.

- **Question-specific remediation with explanation**—In addition to indicating whether or not learners got the question right and what the right answer is, you may want to include an explanation that provides details on the correct answer. With this level of remediation, they see the same answer whether they got it right or wrong.

- **Per correct or incorrect response**—This is a slight variation on the previous method, but with two possible messages: one if the learners answered correctly, and another if they didn't.

- **Per-option remediation**—This is the most detailed form of remediation, with a separate message displayed based on which individual option learners selected, such as one message if they guessed "a" and a different message if they guessed "b," even though both are wrong. This allows you to provide more tailored feedback by addressing what was right or wrong about the specific choice the learners made.

Other Options

A variety of features offer further choices for you and learners on tests and quizzes.

- **More than one attempt allowed**—Based on your programming or authoring tool, you may be able to determine the number of attempts a learner can have for a certain question before being given the answer or being moved on to the next question. This is generally not done with formal assessments but is done when your goal is to give the learner the opportunity to explore and remember.

- **Hints and other help**—When the questioning is for reinforcement, you can provide assistance to the learners if they are struggling. Hints can take the form of a pop-up window that provides relevant text from the course, a link back to where that content was taught (make sure you provide a link to take them back to the question), access to a job aid or reference guide, or some sort of visual clue, such as an arrow or box highlighting the portion of the screen learners should be looking at (used often with diagrams or computer simulations). Hints are sometimes used in formal assessments if the information in the hint would also be available on the job. For example, if a worker can look up an answer in a quick-reference guide on the job, then it might make sense to make that information available in the test.

- **Navigation**—You can set up a relationship between success on a question and navigation. For example, you can choose to set navigation so the learners can't move on until a question is answered correctly. You could set a test so the learners are automatically taken back to the parts of the course that covers what they missed. You could also provide the learners with links to the material for any questions missed and they can choose if they want to go back and review it again. Finally, for compliance or mandated courses, you may want to prevent access to the final test until a learner completes all elements of the course.

Design Tips for Remediation

- **Purpose**—With all of these options available to you, stay true to your purpose. Review your objectives, what you know about your audience, and your goals for testing when making all of these decisions. Don't let the features and options overpower what you are trying to do.

- **Courtesy**—Use respectful, not patronizing, language when providing feedback on incorrect answers.

- **Color coding**—Be careful about using only color to indicate the right or wrong answer. Eight percent of Caucasian men have some sort of color blindness. If you want to use red and green to reinforce, that is fine—just make sure color is not the only indicator. For example, a red "x" and a green checkmark would work well because the color is not critical to getting the message. However, coloring the connecting lines either green or red on a matching exercise would not be understood by someone with red-green color blindness.

- **Usefulness**—If you are going to take the time and effort to script out remediation for each question or even each option, make sure you are providing valuable insight for the learner. If there is a visual display of the right answer (such as the correct answer being bolded) and your text remediation just says the same thing in written form, you are probably wasting development time. Either add something to the message, or rely just on the visual indicators.

Randomization

If you are concerned about the integrity of your test, you may want to include some randomization options, such as mixing up the order of the questions or using different questions each time. This is generally done in two kinds of situations: (1) You want to make sure that if learners need to retake the test, they are truly being retested on the content, rather than being retested on whether they remember what the right and wrong answers were the first time around. (2) You feel there is a reasonable chance the learners will share answers and you want to minimize that as much as possible. Common randomization options are listed, from simplest to most complex:

- **Order of options**—With this type of randomization, all of the same questions appear for each learner each time one of them takes the test. However, each time a question appears, the options are in a different order. For example, on a multiple-choice question the correct answer might be the first choice for one learner and the second choice for another learner. This at least keeps the learner from being able to quickly write down the letter of the correct answer. Sharing and note taking can still occur, but at least the people involved would need to write down the correct concept and not just a letter.

- **Order of questions**—Another method that provides similar benefits is to have the same questions appear for everyone, but have them appear in a different order. Question three for one learner might be question 10 for another learner. Again, this makes it a little more challenging to make notes or share answers.

- **Questions pulled from a question bank**—A higher level of security is created when different questions appear for each person or each time the same person takes a quiz. To do this, you would create more questions than would be used, and the course creates a unique quiz for each person. For example, you may create 20 questions, but each person gets 10. It is harder to share answers when each person is given different questions.

- **Questions pulled per objective from a bank**—If you use the previous method, there's no guarantee that all objectives would be tested. A learner could end up with two questions on objective one and no questions on objective four. One way to guarantee all objectives are met with a question bank is to create a separate bank for each objective. Then one question is pulled from each bank, guaranteeing that all objectives are tested equally. Doing this requires objectives to be identified, several questions to be developed for each objective, those questions to be labeled by objective behind the scenes, and the test engine to be able to pull one (or two, or three, for example) from each objective to create the test. This is one of the most secure self-paced testing methods you can use while still guaranteeing all objectives are tested. This method also requires the most logic to be programmed into your system or be built into your authoring tool.

 Caution: Requirements for Randomization

When looking at authoring tools, talking to development vendors, or working with your own development team, be clear about what type of randomization you want. If you use the term "randomized bank of questions," different people may have different interpretations of what that means. Be specific.

Other Testing Options

Review what you are trying to accomplish and consider any customization to help you meet those objectives. Depending on your tool, there are a number of options for your testing strategy:

- Allow partial credit for any question that requires knowledge of several pieces of information (such as a multiple-choice question with more than one correct answer or a matching question).

- Put one question on a screen, versus having all questions on one scrolling screen.

- Weigh some questions more heavily than others in the overall score.

- Set a time limit to answer the questions. (Be careful about using this option as technical difficulties, physical disabilities, language barriers, or learning disabilities may all affect how long each person takes on a test.)

- Incorporate media elements into the question (audio, video, or graphics).

The Question Creation Process

Writing good questions can easily be the most time-consuming part of building your content. (Ineffective questions can be written very quickly!) To stay on track, be sure to review your objectives carefully and always use them as your guide.

Critical Teaching Point List

One way to stay focused is to forget about the actual questions themselves. Instead, think about the point you want to test or reinforce. Review your objectives (and your content if it already exists) and ask yourself these things:

- If a learner walked away knowing only one thing, what should it be?

- Six months after taking the course, when the learner is on the job on some Tuesday afternoon, what will be the most important things for him or her to remember?

- What information has no room for error?

- What information is likely to cause the most trouble if the learner forgets or misunderstands it?

- What information is likely to create the greatest benefits if the learner implements it correctly?

What information is the most commonly misunderstood? Use the list in Figure 7-7 to determine your most critical teaching points. Once you've done that, you can design questions that test each of the points.

FIGURE 7-7: SAMPLE CRITICAL TEACHING POINT LIST

Objective: Enter an item into the new product database.	
Critical Teaching Point	**Question**
Items will have new item numbers, with 6 digits instead of 5.	
A "7" at the beginning of the item number means it is a corporate brand item.	
There are separate fields for suggested retail price and our actual price.	
New items need to be entered by noon on Wednesday to be sent to the stores in the weekly update.	

From there, turn each of these points into a question that fully tests or reinforces the point. This will help you to avoid testing irrelevant information just because it makes an easy question, ensuring your tests are practical and application based.

The Teaching Point-Idea-Question List

Another way to generate questions is to take the facts generated in Figure 7-7 and then brainstorm ideas, as shown in Figure 7-8, rather than go straight to writing the question.

FIGURE 7-8: TEACHING POINT-IDEA-QUESTION LIST

Objective: Enter an item into the new product database.		
Teaching Point	**Idea**	**Question**
New items need to be entered by noon on Wednesday to be sent to the stores in the weekly update.	Drop-down list with time and day. Calendar/clock where they have to click the right day and time.	

From there, turn each of these ideas into a question that fully tests or reinforces the point. Once the ideas are generated, you could also delegate question writing to someone else.

Common Mistakes With E-Learning Questions

The ability to write good questions shouldn't be much different for e-learning than for traditional instruction. So why then are there so many bad tests out there? Perhaps it is because written tests are not often used in classrooms outside academia. Therefore, experienced instructional designers and trainers may not have much experience creating questions in any training format, e-learning or otherwise.

Here are some common mistakes to avoid:

- **Questions don't test the most important information**—Too often, test questions are built based on what is easy to test. Simple, factual material is the easiest information to create a test question around. However, these factual points may just be supplemental information rather than the important points that deserve reinforcement and assessment.

    Solution: Review your objectives and create a question outline first. Then develop your questions from that list.

 Tips from the Pros: Avoiding Answer Give-Aways

Be careful when using "always" or "never" in a true/false question. Savvy test takers know that "false" is the safe guess in those cases.

If you are going to use "none of the above" or "all of the above" in a multiple-choice question, occasionally make them the wrong answer. Savvy test takers know that often these options are only included when they are the right answer, making them a good guess.

Try to have all the options a similar length. Avoid having one option that is much longer than the others.

Use parallel construction for your options when asking students to complete a sentence in a multiple-choice format. Avoid inconsistencies in subject-verb agreement, singular versus plural, or "a"" versus "an" in answer choices.

- **Questions don't fully test the objective**—Some tests provide just one or two simple questions about single facts in a lesson. Knowing the answer to those one or two questions does not mean the learner has fully achieved the objective.

   Solution: Review your objectives and create a teaching point list first. Then develop your questions from that list.

- **Directions are unclear**—Whether you are using a simple multiple-choice question or a more elaborate drag-and-drop or simulation question, learners could be paralyzed by not understanding how to operate the question. For example, with a multiple-choice question, do they click on the right response or type in a letter? Can they select more than one correct option? Your questions should judge their knowledge of the information, not their ability to figure out how the question works.

   Solution: Remember the skill level of your audience when constructing questions and think like a true beginner when writing instructions for them.

- **Questions have "clues" about the correct answer**—Experienced test takers (and test avoiders) have learned over time how to increase their odds when guessing at a question.
   Solution: Use the tips in the box to make sure you aren't helping out the guessers.

- **Questions don't match the content**—Believe it or not, there are tests out there that test content not covered in the material or content covered in a different module. A more subtle, but just as dangerous, problem is questions that test content to a degree not covered in the module.

   For example, in a class on hiring discrimination, one module covered what the law says about what is considered discrimination. The test asked what interview questions are legal and illegal. Unfortunately, the module never translated the discrimination law to the types of questions that were or were not appropriate in an interview.

   Solution: Have clearly defined objectives and questions before you develop your content. Have a full review of the course done by someone not involved in the development process.

- **Questions have unclear answers**—Because not everything in the world is black and white, it can be challenging to create objective multiple-choice and true/false questions for every type of content—and, yet, that is what some developers try to do. Because of this, some questions are, well, questionable! There may be incorrect options that really are correct in the right situation. And yet, because it wasn't what was taught in the class, the option is deemed incorrect. Because there may not be an instructor to clarify the answers, you could be causing confusion in the minds of learners and inadvertently labeling a positive idea as a negative one.

   Solution: Try to argue with your own questions to see if there might be a different perspective. Make sure you aren't marking something as incorrect just because it is not the focus of your lesson.

Been There; Done That: Easy-to-Write Questions vs. Good Questions

Superficial facts and trivia make easy-to-write questions. However, those items are rarely important enough to reinforce. Back in the early 2000s, there was an online course created to teach about the Internet. The quiz at the end asked questions such as the year the Internet was created. That's an easy multiple-choice question to write. However, when was the learner ever likely to need that information in his or her life? A better question might have been about what equipment the learner would need to access the Internet. Focus your questions on what will help the learners meet the goals of the course—not what will help them win prizes on game shows.

 Dive Deeper

Telling Ain't Training by Harold D. Stolovitch and Erica J. Keeps

Interactions

There is a difference between training and a keynote speech. The first is generally a two-way, back-and-forth exchange, and the second is one-way communication. Similarly, there is a difference between e-learning and e-reading. Effective e-learning provides interaction for the learner, while e-reading is a more passive activity.

Just as a classroom training session can be made more effective by questions, activities, games, and discussions, so can your e-learning.

Reasons for Interaction

As with any element of the design phase, you'll want to start out by understanding your purpose. Games, activities, and interactions can be used for:

- reinforcing understanding
- application of the material
- retention
- practice
- motivation to learn
- fun.

Types of Interactions

Based on what you are trying to accomplish, there are many options at your disposal.

Offline Activities

Offline activities are any activities that do not rely solely on the course. While the instructions and the assignment may reside in the course, the learners would perform the offline activity outside of the course. Feedback wouldn't be provided to them unless they submitted their work to an instructor. This opens up a number of additional options, such as:

- **Reflection questions**—These give the learners something to think about and reflect on after the course. For example: "Think about the best teacher you ever had and jot down some of the things you liked best about him or her. Then review the list and see how many of the same qualities hold true for a good supervisor."

- **Internet research**—Ask the learners to do a bit of research on their own. For example, ask them to look up the origin of the Section 508 guidelines for e-learning.

- **Software application assignments**—Provide the files and instructions for learners to perform a software task; then have them complete the task on their own version of the software, instead of in the course itself.

- **Traditional homework assignments and projects**—If appropriate, you can assign anything you might assign in a classroom environment.

Collaborative Activities

These entail the involvement of an instructor, a mentor, or other class members. They require that other learners are going through the same course at the same time, but they allow for the type of discussion and feedback that can be so useful in a classroom environment. Examples include:

- threaded discussions or forums

- email discussions

- group projects

- surveys and polls.

Simple Activities in the Course

Most authoring tools allow for a wide variety of interactions, such as:

- reinforcement questions (multiple choice, matching, drag and drop)

- click-to-reveal activities (any interaction that requires learner involvement to display on-screen information, such as rollovers and pop-ups)

- situational scenarios (more elaborate forms of questions where the fact or concept is put in a job-specific context and the learner has to make decisions about a realistic situation based on the course content).

Advanced Online Activities (Asynchronous)

Advanced activities include simulations and games, both discussed earlier in the chapter. Advanced interactions can help your learners delve deeper into the content and practice using the information they are being taught. These advanced activities can also add significantly to your schedule and budget.

Classifying Levels of Interactivity

Whether you are determining cost and budget at the beginning of a project or making specific decisions about interactivity during the design phase, it can be helpful to use a classification system for the levels of interactivity. These levels can help make sure everyone is operating with the same understanding.

The most commonly used system for classifying interactivity comes from the U.S. Department of Defense.

Level I: Passive

In this level, the learner acts merely as a receiver of information. The learner may read text on the screen as well as view graphics, illustrations, and charts. The learner may interact simply by using navigational buttons to move forward or back through the program.

Level II: Limited Interaction

In this second level, the learner makes simple responses to instructional cues. As in Level I, there may be multiple choice exercises, pop-ups, rollovers, or simple animations. Level II adds a component of scenario-based multiple choice and column matching related to the text and graphic presentation.

Level III: Complex Interaction

Here, the learner makes multiple, varied responses to cues. In addition to the types of responses in Level II, complex interactions may require text entry boxes and manipulation of graphic objects to test the assessment of the information presented.

Level IV: Real-time Interaction

Real-time interaction creates a training session that involves a life-like set of complex cues and responses in this last level. The learner is engaged in a simulation that exactly mirrors the work situation.

Tips From the Pros: Designing Interactions

- Start with a list of points to be reinforced. Interactions can be the most time consuming and expensive part of e-learning development—so make sure you have a point. You can use the same list you created for your questions. If the points are worth testing, they are worth reinforcing.
- Consider some sort of interaction every five to seven screens at a minimum.
- Make instructions clear.
- Ensure your training objective is met. Don't get too carried away with the fun factor.
- Be sure most of your interactions get the learner thinking, rather than having all of them simply require the learner to click a button to learn more.
- Consider the shelf-life of the material before designing an interaction. Information that might need to be updated periodically may be a good choice for a simple question rather than an elaborate simulation—to keep maintenance costs down.

Summary

Testing and interactivity are what keep your e-learning engaging and effective. Keep in mind that these elements often take the most creativity to design and the most time and money to create. So always make sure that they are designed in a way that meets your needs and your learners' needs.

8

THE DESIGN PHASE: MEDIA, INTERFACE, AND NAVIGATION

With your testing and assessments planned out, you can now turn your attention to the look and feel of the course as well as how the learners will get around.

Media

Your media choices will be made based on a combination of technical factors, audience factors, and learning issues.

Graphics and Animations

Graphics and animations in an e-learning course can be either decorative or informative. Decorative graphics should be used sparingly so they don't compete with the content. When done properly, a graphic can be a great way to communicate a lot of information in a very small space. A graphic can also set a tone or evoke an emotion.

You may want to designate an overall style for the graphics based on the audience (busy executives in a conservative organization versus sales people in a casual organization) or the mood (a harassment prevention course versus product knowledge on an exciting new technology product). For example, would it be better to use stock photography, actual photos from the work environment, clip art, cartoons, or custom graphics—even custom-created characters?

If there are limits on file size, pixel size, or file format, be sure to define those at this stage of the project.

Audio

Whether or not to include audio in your e-learning course can turn into a great debate. There are pros and cons and many ways to approach it.

These are some reasons to use audio:

- **Reinforcement and retention**—When information is presented using several different senses or experiences, retention is improved.

- **Language and literacy barriers**—Some learners who may struggle with a text-based course may do better with audio information.

- **An engaging experience**—The addition of media such as audio can mean a richer experience for some learners.

These are reasons to avoid using (or at least relying on) audio:

- **Budget limitations**—Professional-sounding audio can be expensive to produce and expensive to maintain when there are changes.

- **Technology restrictions**—The audience may not have speakers or head phones and sound cards.

- **Environment restrictions**—Background noise in the learners' environment could interfere with them listening to the course, or the audio in the course could interfere with what is going on in the background.

- **Disability issues**—A portion of your audience may have hearing impairments. While this wouldn't prevent you from using audio, it would require you to provide a text alternative, such as closed captioning.

To give the learner the most flexibility, consider including an audio on/off selector; volume control within the course window; and pause, stop, and replay buttons. If you include an on/off selector, make sure there is another way the learner can get the content, such as a transcript.

Video

Video can be a great option to demonstrate a procedure or add a human touch such as with a video testimonial or role play. However, video can be very expensive to develop and has large file sizes, especially if the playback quality of the video is important.

The same pros and cons that apply to audio also apply to video. Because you are adding the visual element, consider the monitor quality and size, as well as any visual impairments of your audience members when choosing video.

Interface and Navigation

Have you ever gotten lost in a website and couldn't figure out how to get back to where you started? Have you ever suffered through a presentation that used every single color, font, and animation available? In each of these cases, you've suffered from poor design—either in form or in function.

The interface design for your e-learning course includes the graphic design elements, the special features and functions, and the navigation. It is the structure that houses the content. Making good choices about your interface design and navigation can mean the difference between an enjoyable, effective learning session and a frustrating waste of time.

When thinking about interface design, consider each word individually.

- **Interface**—You are creating the interface between the learners and the content. The learners are trying to retrieve information, and they use the interface to do so. Therefore, your interface design should be structured, logical, consistent, and orderly, so the learners know where they are and what they should do to get the results they want.

- **Design**—For the vast majority of your users, the e-learning course will be a visual experience. Therefore, the course should be designed in a visually pleasing way that sets the right tone and supports the message without interfering with it.

 Tips from the Pros: Marketing Knows Best

Have your interface design approved by your marketing department and anyone else who might have strong preferences about fonts, colors, and logo usage.

Graphic Design

In a perfect world, every e-learning development team would work with a professional graphic artist for their course design. However, this task often falls to those without formal training or experience. Fortunately, effective e-learning interface design is very similar to effective website design.

While it is impossible to cover everything you might need to know about good graphic design, here are a few highlights to make sure you are on the right track.

Fonts

- Never sacrifice legibility for creativity.

- Pick no more than three fonts or font styles for your course. Use one for headings, one for body text, and one for special attention, such as titles or warnings.

- Make sure your text font is easy to read. If you can, stay with body text between 10 and 12 points. Select a simple font such as Verdana.

- Apply no more than one (maybe two) formatting styles to any element. Bold, italic, underlined, colored, shadowed type is overkill.

Colors

- Keep it simple. Select a neutral background color and two accent colors. Use the accent colors for headings, borders, and graphs. A unified color scheme makes your work look more professional.

- Have your on-screen text black or dark blue if it appears on a light background or white or off-white if it is on a dark background. Make sure there is enough contrast between the text and the background so it can be read clearly. (Again, never sacrifice legibility for creativity.)

- Avoid background patterns. They cause too much eye strain.

Page Layout

- Create different page layouts for different screen types. For example, try one design for module titles, another for text with a graphic, one for a large graphic with little or no text, and one for a lot of text without a graphic. But be willing to stray from established designs so you can focus on what's best for a given piece of content.

- Keep your design clean and simple. Provide for adequate page margins as well as space between on-screen elements (such as the text and a graphic).

- When creating your overall interface design (header, footer, menu), be sure to use space-efficient elements so you have enough real estate on the page to fit a sufficient amount of content.

Buttons

- Label all buttons with text so there is no question what they are for.

- When possible, use web standards for buttons, providing a different look when a button is active or inactive, rolled over, or clicked.

- Don't be afraid to have a little fun with the buttons. You have some room to be creative here as long as there is no question what the buttons are for.

Tips from the Pros: Design Double-Check

Questions to ask yourself to avoid a major design blunder:
- Can I read everything?
- If I had to look at this for an hour straight, would it give me a headache?
- Can I tell what everything is for?
- Does it scream "professionalism" or "lemonade stand"?

Navigation Options

"Where am I?" "Are we there yet?" "I think I'm lost." "How do I get out of here?" No, these aren't just phrases heard from the kids in the back seat of the car on a long road trip. These are things your learners might be thinking as they move around your course. Setting up clear and purposeful navigation will help your learners move efficiently through your course.

Fixed Versus Flexible Navigation

Start by making some fundamental decisions about who is in control. And once again, go back to your objectives, business need, and audience analysis to make that decision.

Flexible navigation allows the learners to move freely around the course, taking only the sections they want, in the order they want. This method is best used when you have an audience who is motivated and can make sound judgments about what they need to learn, or information that is helpful but not required.

Forced navigation requires the learners to complete the course in a preset format, without the ability to move around. This method is best when you have an audience that is required to take the training but doesn't really want to, one that doesn't have a good grasp of what they do or don't need to learn, or mandated information.

You can create variations and hybrids of these two models. For example:
- Loosen up fixed navigation by requiring a set path through the course until it is completed and passed and then releasing the navigation so the learner can move around freely for review, refresher, or performance support.
- Tighten fixed navigation by requiring that every element on a page be completed (such as the audio playing completely, all rollovers or hot spots accessed) before the learner can select the Next button.

Choose your strategy carefully. Too much control given to a learner in the wrong situation can result in very little learning taking place. If you take too much control from learners who can work independently, they can get very frustrated when the course takes longer than it needs to.

The Great Debate: Locking Down Course Navigation

Many e-learning designers feel strongly that you should never lock down the navigation on a course. They argue that adult learners learn best when they have full control over their learning. Others believe that the organization's need for the learning to take place outweighs the individual preferences of the learner. This is especially true with safety, compliance, or other mandated topics. At the end of the day, you need to answer a simple question. If you allow learners to skip content, some of them will. Is that OK? If it is, then consider having open navigation. If it is not, then perhaps you'll want to lock down navigation.

Progress and Location Indicators

Progress and location indicators help learners see the big picture of the course and help them know what to expect.

Menu Options

If learners are able to move freely around the course, then a menu is usually the tool that lets them do that. Even if the learner will not have control of the navigation, it might still be useful for the learners to see a menu for the course so they know what to expect.

Some authoring tools allow the menu to be visible at all times. In other cases, the menu is a click away, such as in a pop-up box, a drop-down menu, or a sliding side panel. Another helpful option is to include a Home button that lets the learner return to the beginning of the course or module, if desired.

Try to avoid going more than three levels deep with menu options. For example, you may have a course made up of modules (Level 1). The modules contain lessons (Level 2). The lessons contain pages (Level 3). If you go too deep into the hierarchy, the learners can easily lose track of where they are in the course.

Title Placement

When you are several levels deep in a course, it is nice to have a reminder of where you are. This helps the learners put the information they are seeing into context with all the information in the course. One way to assist with this is to display the course, module, or lesson name at all times. This takes up precious real estate, but can be designed to be unobtrusive.

FIGURE 8-1: EXAMPLE OF A BREADCRUMB, OR COURSE TITLE PLACEMENT

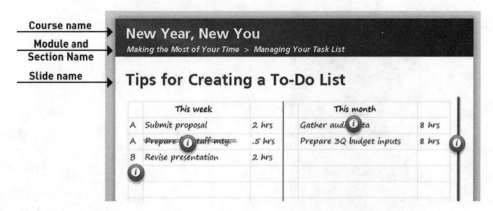

Page Counters

Page counters (*page 3 of 10*, for example) provide a useful courtesy to your learners. As they begin a course, module, or lesson, they will have a good idea of how long they need to be able to commit to the course. You can choose to have one set of numbering for the course across all modules and lessons, or you can choose to start renumbering for each lesson.

Bookmarking and Progress Indicators

Bookmarks allow the learners to come back to the point where they last left off. Then when they return, they are asked if they want to pick up where they left off.

FIGURE 8-2: EXAMPLE OF A BOOKMARK

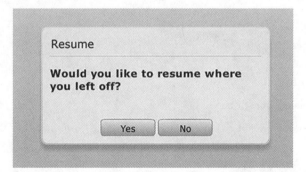

Progress indicators generally appear on the course menu and indicate which sections have been started, completed, or passed by the learner. Many authoring tools provide this logic automatically. With others, it must be set up manually.

FIGURE 8-3: SHOWING PROGRESS ON A COURSE MENU

In both cases, the course sends the bookmark and progress data to the LMS to save until the next time the learner launches the course. If you are not using an LMS, the information can be saved in the browser using cookies. This works only if the learner comes back to the course using the same computer, sign-on, and browser.

Special Features and Functions

Based on your audience, objectives, and programming options, you may want to include some or all of these course features:

- glossary
- help
- how to use this course
- FAQs (frequently asked questions)
- reference documents
- job aids
- index
- searchable text
- handouts
- note-taking screens.

One of the best ways to decide what you want to include in your course is to review as many free online samples as you can find. But remember, just because you can do something doesn't mean you should. Keep your objectives and your audience at the forefront at all times. Make sure the technology supports the learning and doesn't overpower it.

The Design Document

By now you've made a lot of decisions about how your courses should be designed and developed. These decisions now need to be documented and agreed upon. This information generally takes the form of a design document.

Much of what is included in the design document relates to the instructional design decisions covered in the previous chapters. The design document may also include the objectives and instructional strategies settled on during the first part of the design phase. You may also choose to separate out some of the writing and graphic design issues into a style guide. The names and numbers of the documents don't really matter—what matters is that you make purposeful decisions and document them so everyone can work together.

The design document will be used by writers, instructional designers, editors, proofreaders, artists, and programmers. You may also use the design document to help you select an authoring tool or to help you write an RFP for a custom content development vendor.

Other elements to be included in a design document, such as the standards and storyboard information, relate to production. The storyboarding process is explained in chapter 9.

Refer to the sample outline in Figure 8-4 for some suggestions on what to include in your design document.

FIGURE 8-4: SAMPLE DESIGN DOCUMENT OUTLINE

Background

Briefly describe the overall training project, including the business need.

Rationale for E-Learning

Explain why e-learning is being used as a training element. Include whether it will be used for initial training, refresher training, performance support, or other purpose.

E-Learning Environment

Business Description
Describe the business in terms of number of locations, number of employees and culture.

Audience Description
Describe audience members in terms of position, experience on the job, experience using computers, age, turnover, and any other factors relevant to the training.

Technology Description
Describe the systems used for hosting and viewing the courseware, including restrictions.

FIGURE 8-4: SAMPLE DESIGN DOCUMENT OUTLINE (CONTINUED)

Content Structure

Course Objectives
Give a list of objectives with information about where they should go in the course.

Course Taxonomy

Describe how the course will be broken up: modules, lessons, or other units.

Module Structure and Screen Sequence

Describe the standard introductory, content, and closing screens as they should be used for the whole course and for individual modules.

Seq. No.	Screen Type	Description
Screens for the course as a whole		
1.	Welcome screen for course	Visually interesting with minimum text
2.	Course Overview *(may be more than one screen)*	Gets the learner interested in the course. Explains high-level concept of training and terminal objectives.
3.	How to Use This Course *(may be more than one screen)*	Instructs learner how to operate and navigate the course.
Screens for each individual module		
1.	Overview of Module	Gets the learner excited about learning that procedure. Lists enabling objectives.
2.	Instructional/procedural frames	Provides training content.
3.	Summary or end of topic frame	Congratulates the learner. Reinforces most important points. Introduces and navigates to the guided practice.
4.	Practice Overview	Provides instructions for the solo practice. Lists a refresher of the steps.
5.	Practice Steps	Provides sample data and gives feedback for each step. Last feedback branches to re-start the practice if at least two steps were missed

Instructional Strategies

Presentation Materials
Describe what types of instructional materials will be used in the course. For example, video, audio, text narration, or diagrams.

Practice and Assessment
Describe how the content will be practiced or how you will assess the learners' learning.

Compliance Considerations

Describe if the course will need to be SCORM, AICC, xAPI or Section 508 compliant.

Testing and Assessments

Question Types
Describe the types of questions that can or should be used in the course, such as multiple choice, matching, among others.

Placement
Explain if you will be using pretests, post-tests, or individual questions embedded throughout the content.

Remediation
Describe the type of remediation you will be using throughout the course.

Randomization
Explain any randomization options you plan to use, including the order of options, order of questions, or the use of a test bank.

FIGURE 8-4: SAMPLE DESIGN DOCUMENT OUTLINE (CONTINUED)

Interactions

Interaction Types
Describe the type of interactions, such as offline activities, that can be used in the course.

Media

Graphics and Animations
Describe such things as the overall graphics style, limits of file size, and file format.

Audio
If audio will be used, explain how it will be built into the course (for example, if it will be optional).

Video
If video will be part of the course, explain how it will be used.

Interface and Navigation

Graphic Design
Describe such things as what fonts and colors will be used, the page layout, and what buttons will look like.

Navigation Options
Explain how the learner will access the courses and move around between different sections. Designate the use of fixed versus flexible navigation.

Progress and Location Indicators
Describe what the learners will see as they use the course. Describe menu options, title placement, page counters, and bookmarking.

Special Features and Functions
Explain any special features for the course, such as glossary, help, or FAQs.

Storyboards

Format
Explain what format will be used for the storyboards (such as Word or PowerPoint).

Naming Conventions
Explain how the module documents should be named (both the storyboard document and the course files). Describe how the storyboards should be numbered (for example, increments of five).

Styles
If styles will be used in the storyboards, designate what styles should be used for each part of the storyboard. For example, you may want all screen titles to be formatted with Heading 1 style and all paragraph headings with Heading 2 style.

Character Restrictions
If there are limits to the number of words, lines, or characters for any individual element in the course, specify that here. For example, you may be able to fit 15 lines of text using a two-inch column, or you may have a limit for 40 characters for a module title. (This is especially important with form-based authoring tools.)

Writing Standards and Conventions

Terminology
Outline any special terminology requirements for the project. For example, do you want to use the phrase "Click Next" or "Click Forward"? Do you have a preference about computer terminology? Should employees be called associates? Employees?

Writing Style
Describe the tone, style, and targeted education level for the writing.

FIGURE 8-4: SAMPLE DESIGN DOCUMENT OUTLINE (CONTINUED)

Grammar and Formatting Standards
Designate what style guide or grammar reference will be used (for example, *Gregg Reference Manual*, *Chicago Manual of Style*, or *Microsoft Manual of Style*). You may instead choose to spell out the specific grammatical and formatting standards you want to use in the course, or anything you want to do that is contrary to the style guide you have chosen.

Interactions
Describe how each interaction type should be worded and any restrictions for each type (such as the number of options possible for a multiple-choice question).

Assessments
Describe how tests should be worded or formatted.

Additional Sections
Provide additional sections for any other part of the course that should have set content, language, or formatting, such as captions, headings, opening and closing screens, objectives, instructions, and feedback.

Development Process

Project Management
Describe how the project will be tracked.

Interface and Prototype Development
Describe how the interface and prototype will be developed, what content will be used, and what, if anything, can be done before it is finalized.

Storyboard Development
Include relevant information about source materials, subject matter experts, and philosophy to be used for the storyboard development.

Storyboard Review
Outline who will be reviewing the storyboards at which phases of development and what they will be looking for (and what might be considered an out-of-scope change).

Graphics Development
Describe technical, artistic, and instructional design issues for the use of graphics not already covered.

Online Draft Development and Review
Outline who will be reviewing the online draft at which phases of development and what they will be looking for (and what might be considered an out-of-scope change).

Systems Integration
Explain the steps to be taken to ensure the course works properly on the target systems.

Summary

The more you can plan and prepare before you begin your development, the more effective your course will be, and the more efficient your production effort will become. Document decisions along the way and remember to always stay true to your audience and objectives. Ensure that the technology supports the learning and doesn't detract from it.

9

THE DEVELOPMENT PHASE: WRITING THE COURSE

Once you have designed your course, how are you going to get those ideas to come to life? How will you capture what elements you want on each slide, and how it will all function? It is easy to be overwhelmed with your course's technical possibilities.

Whether you are working with a developer who will build the course from your instructions, or you are taking care of everything yourself, it is time to organize and write your content. This chapter walks you through the process of getting your information and ideas in writing so you can make technology meet the objectives of your course.

Working With Storyboards

Storyboards are the blueprints for your course. You can use them to work out the details of the content, get approval from stakeholders before assembly begins, and provide direction to developers, artists, and other team members on how to build the course to your specifications.

What Is a Storyboard?

In the 1920s, Walt Disney Studios started using storyboards with drawings for the scenes of the early *Steamboat Willie* cartoons. Major movie makers still use them today as an aid in creating the vision of the storylines in modern films. The storyboard system has grown and is now used in business for such things as project planning, manufacturing process design, and training course development.

The word *storyboard* can mean two different things in the e-learning world. It can mean a high-level flowchart of the course, or it can be a detailed description of all content and programming. You may want to create both.

The high-level storyboard is useful for mapping out how many screens you may devote to a subject, where the activities will go, and how complex logic will work, among other things.

FIGURE 9-1: SAMPLE HIGH-LEVEL STORYBOARD

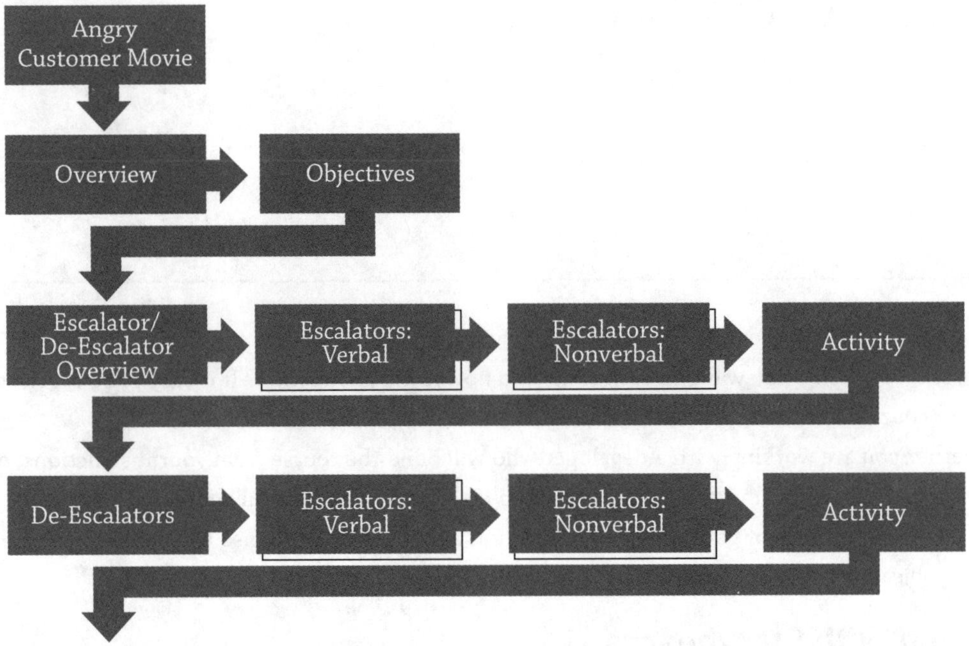

The rest of this chapter focuses on the detailed storyboard. This type of storyboard:

- **Contains your course content**—This includes the text that will be on each screen, as well as all the interactions, questions, and graphics.

- **Provides directions to the developer or artists**—Developers and artists need to know exactly what the developer wants the course to look like and how it should function. The storyboard does this. For example, the developer will need to know where the "Next" button should take the learner so the path can be programmed properly. Note: The developer is the person who assembles the course in the chosen authoring tool.

- **Creates the vision for the course**—The instructional strategies and course features outlined in the design document now come to life. The storyboard writer provides the information and instructions that the developer uses to create the course.

- **Reduces rework**—Every course goes through review and revision cycles. If the first review was done on a fully authored version of the course, you'd have a lot of expensive and time-consuming changes to make. If the reviews are done on the storyboards, the changes can be made before the media and programming work get started.

FIGURE 9-2: SAMPLE STORYBOARD AND RESULTING COURSE PAGE

24	Law	Law Enforcement	
On-screen Text		**Narration**	
What do you do? A. You provide him with the files but ask him to keep them in the registration area, in case a staff member needs them. **B. You politely ask the police officer to wait while you go and get your supervisor.**		A uniformed police offer approaches you at the registration desk. He shows you his badge. "I'm with the Springfield County Sheriff's Department, and we have reason to believe a suspect in a murder attempt is in your shelter. We need to see your records and walk around a little bit to determine if he's here." What do you do?	
Graphic Suggestions			
Lobby background Police officer			
Programming Notes			
Correct/Not Quite feedback indicator, followed by this text: The rule here is actually very simple. A registration worker should never share records with anyone, unless directed to do so by a supervisor. Go get your supervisor to work out a solution with the officer. In this case, the supervisor will most likely accommodate his request because it is a matter of public safety and imminent danger.			

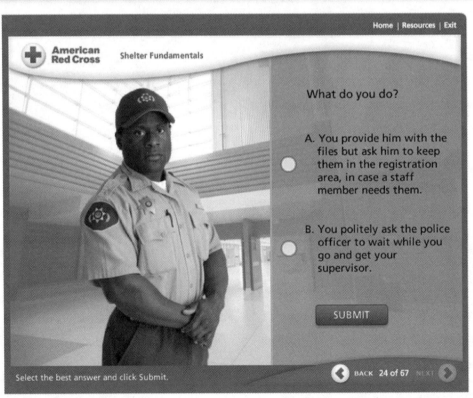

Image provided courtesy of American Red Cross.

Elements of Storyboards

There isn't one specific way a storyboard should look. A storyboard could be a drawing (similar to a comic strip) or could be only text. It could be written on a piece of paper or could be done in templates on the computer that look much like the interface that will be used for the course. There are, however, certain things that should be included in a good storyboard.

Page Names and Numbers

When you are working with storyboards, it is important that you and any of your developers are able to follow the blueprint of your course. In addition, you'll need to keep track of many individual files that make up each course and screen (for example, graphics and page files). To guarantee that everyone knows what to do and where to find the different elements, it is best to come up with standards about how to name and number everything from pages to graphics to audio files. Here are some tips to help you when designating page numbers:

- **If you have different types of screens or screen layouts, include that in your numbering conventions.** For example, if at the end of each section you have decided to include test questions, your test question page numbers may all be in the 200s. That way, any time you see a number that is in the 200 range, you and your team members will automatically know test questions are included. This is also helpful if you need to quickly and easily pull out all of the test-question storyboards for editing purposes.

- **Begin your page number with something that represents the project, course, or module you are working on.** For example, if you are writing a training course on how to use Microsoft Word, you may want to start the page number with MSW. If it is the second module in the course, then the page number might be MSW-B-05. This is helpful for organization if you are working on multiple courses.

- **Avoid using spaces in any file names.** Some web-based programs do not handle spaces well. Instead, use a hyphen (-) or underscore (_) if you need to separate words.

- **Consider using keywords instead of numbers.** Your storyboards may start with easy-to-understand sequential numbering. But once you start adding, deleting, and rearranging pages during the review process, the old page numbers can get confusing. Consider adding a short, unique keyword to each slide. Even if the page number changes, the keyword wouldn't. That way, you know that MSW-B-05-Style is for the screen on styles, even if it ends up moving around.

On-Screen Text

The text can be the easiest part of the storyboard to write—or the most difficult. This depends greatly on the complexity of the course, the types of interactions you are developing, and your natural writing style.

Text in your storyboard should include:

- **learning points**. The text of your storyboard should include information that supports your learning objectives.

- **learner instructions**. These instructions tell the learner how to move from screen to screen in the course. For example, if you have a "Next" button in the interface, you may want to tell learners to "Click NEXT to continue" after they have read the page. Or, if you have included an interaction or question, you will want to explain how to use it.

- **alt-text**. If you have ever put your mouse over a graphic on a website and saw a small pop-up box that describes the graphic, that's alt-text. Alt-text is useful for anyone using screen-reader technology due to visual impairments. If you want to attach alt-text to your graphics, include that text in your storyboard.

The text is not limited to the static text fields. Interactions can also include text. Rollovers are great ways to add learning text. For example, if you are developing a computer course, you may want to create rollovers that highlight the main parts of a window in the application. Each hotspot or rollover could include valuable text about that part of the application.

Media Elements

Each storyboard should contain information about the graphics, audio, video, simulation, or other media files to be included. If the media element already exists, you can simply tell the developer the name of the file to use. However, you can also use the storyboard to provide instructions or guidance if a media element needs to be found or created from scratch.

Audio Narration Script

If you are including audio in your course, you would typically include the narration script, and possibly special instructions. If each screen has audio that is an exact match to the text, then the audio instructions can be very brief. You would need to indicate:

- how to pronounce any words that might be unfamiliar to the person doing the voice work

- how you want any acronyms, initialisms, or abbreviations to be read

- how to handle any special screen types—for example, for a question screen, do you want the question read along with all the options and the remediation? For a rollover screen, do you want to tie audio to each of the pop-up options, or just the instructions?

- what tone you want—for example, if you have characters in a scenario, you might want to indicate if they are upset or soft spoken.

Video

If you are creating custom video for your course, you will need to script what needs to be said, as well as what the learner should see. For this, it would be good to think about how Disney would use a storyboard. You may want to sketch your ideas about actions and scenes first, and then later provide a detailed script and description of the action and angles, for example. The more time you put into the storyboard for the video footage, the less time consuming (and therefore less expensive) the video shoot and editing process will be.

Graphics

If you will be using existing graphics such as clip-art and stock photography collections or graphics available in the public domain, describe in your storyboards what the artist, researcher, or developer should look for. For example:

> A photo of a man in business casual clothing talking on the phone with an agitated look on his face.

If a custom graphic is needed, explain the graphic in detail and possibly provide a sketch.

In some cases, you may want to find the actual graphic to be used and paste it into the storyboard for approval, rather than wait until the online draft phase.

Other Media Elements

Based on the design of your course, you may need to provide other instructions unique to the features you will be including. For example, if you will be using software simulations, include the directions for what the simulation should do.

File Types and Naming Conventions

You may want to include details about the sizes and types of files to be used in the course. This can often be done in the design document if the information is universal for the whole course. If it is likely to vary from screen to screen, then include the details in the storyboard. For example, you may want to specify whether a graphic should be in JPG or GIF format—and maybe even specify the pixel size of the graphic. You also have the option of leaving that up to the artist or developer.

Programming Instructions

The programming instructions show a developer how to take the learner from screen to screen during the course and how each individual screen operates. Developers follow the instructions you give to ensure that the screen order and navigation are the way you intended. You may want to provide detailed instructions, stipulate what template to use, or use a combined method, where you only put in instructions if you need to deviate from the norm. For example, only describe what the "Next" button does if it does something other than go to the "Next" slide in the storyboards.

Navigation

Let the developer know the sequence of the screens and where the interface buttons should take the end user. Include any special requirements for any of the buttons as well. For example:

> Next button: goes to screen OL-205.
> —or—
> Next button: inactive until question is answered correctly, then goes to OL-205.

Links, Documents, or Special Features

Include any special instructions about documents to be attached to a page, hyperlinks to be included, or any other special features based on the design of your course. For example, if your course has a glossary and there is a word on the page that is in the glossary, you may want to include a hyperlink. You would indicate this on the storyboard. For example:

> At the end of the on-screen text, include a hyperlink to the company's ethics policy.
> Text for hyperlink: View our company's policy.
> Document to link: R:\Policies and Procedures\Ethics.doc
> Have document open up in a separate browser window.

Interactions

When you are storyboarding interactions, it is important to be very precise in your explanation of what you want. Developers will often be creating interactions from scratch rather than from a template, so you will want to make sure you explain the interaction, including the teaching text and the instructions that should be given to the learner. Conversely, if you have a good relationship with your developer and a flexible client, you may just want to describe the general goal and the specific text, and let the developer decide whether to use, for example, a drop-down list or a drag-and-drop activity.

Questions

Instructions about questions include several elements:

- **Question type**—Is it multiple choice or true/false, for example?
- **Question and the options**—This includes the on-screen text for the question and whatever answer choices are provided for the learner.
- **On-screen instructions**—This is the text that tells the learner how to operate the question. For example, if it is a matching question, is the learner supposed to click on the correct answer or drag an imaginary line?
- **Remediation**—This is the text that appears when the learner answers correctly or incorrectly.

- **Programming instructions**—These are any special guidelines about how the question should be set up. For example, the number of attempts a learner can have or if the question is tied to a specific objective in a randomized bank of questions.

Storyboard Templates

Storyboard templates are a great way to make sure all of the elements you need for your storyboard are included. Templates can be outline based, form based, or give a visual representation of your course. They ensure that the format for your screen types is consistent throughout your course. Some course designs may require custom templates, or you may be able to find templates that have already been created.

If your authoring tool does not come with storyboard templates, then you'll want to decide what tool to use for storyboarding. Some tools that are good for developing storyboards are Word, PowerPoint, and Visio.

FIGURE 9-3: STORYBOARD TEMPLATE

Screen Title		Screen Type	Screen Number	Keyword
Onscreen Text			**Narration**	
Graphic Suggestions				
Programming Notes				

It is helpful to create a template for each different screen type you intend to use. These types might include, but are not limited to, layouts for:

- introduction
- objective

- standard teaching screen

- demonstration

- rollovers

- hot spots

- video clips

- practice

- each question type

- summary.

Organizing Your Content

Now that you know what belongs in a storyboard, how do you gather and organize the information? Most English writing instructors advise learners to outline their thoughts and ideas before they start writing. Here is how to outline information in storyboard fashion:

- **Develop your objectives**. This was done during the design phase (chapter 6).

- **Create taxonomy and outline**. This was also done during the design phase (chapter 6).

- **Write your test questions**. This was done during the design phase (chapter 7).

- **Write the main point on each storyboard**. Once you have outlined your course at a high level, divide your screens or pages by objective or main point. This may seem like an easy step to skip. But because of the time and effort needed to create each and every screen, it will be very important that your writing is clear, organized, and succinct. Sketching out the main point that goes on each screen will help you stay targeted and will help you keep development time and costs under control. A high-level storyboard might be useful here.

- **Add supporting points**. This takes the information to a deeper level than your outline.

- **Go back and write the actual text**. The information you have gathered from your topic research, subject matter experts, and various documentation can now be added to the storyboards.

- **Add the interactions and reinforcement questions**. The interactions you create should support the learning goal.

- **Add navigation instructions**. Include the navigation instructions on each storyboard.

- **Write special feature pages**. You may have designed special feature buttons, such as glossary, FAQ, and job aids. Write storyboards for each of those buttons so they will contain the information you want.

Throughout the process, make sure you are using good instructional design strategies. To help guide you through this process, periodically look back at all the information you gathered and decisions you made during the analysis and design phases.

Converting Existing Content

When you are converting existing content from instructor-led training (ILT) to e-learning, you will find a new set of challenges. It is normal to think that if you already have a course designed for the classroom that it could quickly and easily be converted to e-learning with little or no additional effort. Unfortunately, this is rarely the case. Here are some special concerns when converting existing content.

Course Length

Because of the cost of e-learning development, you'll want to make sure to include only the elements that are truly necessary for the learning to take place. You don't want to strip out content to save time and money, but you will want to look at the entire program carefully and possibly eliminate some of the "nice-to-know" information. Typically, an e-learning course will be half the length of an ILT training—without cutting content.

Anticipating Questions

When creating a self-paced course without an instructor, you might need to be more thorough in your explanation of some areas. Learners taking an e-learning course don't have the benefit of asking an instructor clarifying questions. Make sure you give important information and adequate explanations up front so the learner can meet learning goals. One way of making sure you answer the learners' questions up front would be to ask the classroom instructors what questions they typically receive during a class session.

Including *All* the Content

Sometimes the most valuable information a learner gets from ILT comes from the instructor, rather than the written materials. For example, if a PowerPoint presentation is your only documentation, you may have only about 20 to 40 percent of the content taught. Some of the best teaching points can come from an off-the-cuff story told by an instructor. So if you are using the written materials alone to develop your e-learning course, you may be missing important information. You may want to interview instructors to see what personal stories or special information they are giving their classes that may not be included in the written materials.

Interactions

Any good classroom training includes interactions where the learners have a chance to think, reflect, respond, and process. Some of those activities might work in an online environment, but some of them won't. You will need to decide how to make sure your online learners get the same level of engagement, practice, and application as your classroom learners.

Informal Changes to the ILT Materials

Over time, instructors learn what does and doesn't work in the classroom. They may have made a number of changes to content, format, or teaching strategies based on feedback they've received—as well as from their own judgment. These changes may not have ever been incorporated into the ILT materials, but may be something you want to look into prior to developing the e-learning class. Just because something is written in the ILT manuals, doesn't mean it was a successful element of the classroom learning experience.

If you have existing courseware, you should be able to develop your e-learning in less time than if you are starting from scratch, but realize that it will not be a straight conversion. You will need to put extra thought and perhaps extra research into the process.

Summary

Storyboarding provides the blueprint for your course. Make sure you include all of the necessary elements so your blueprint is complete. Whether you are having others develop your course or are building it yourself, using storyboards helps to organize your content and ensure that everyone is working toward the same goal.

10

THE DEVELOPMENT PHASE: PUTTING THE COURSE TOGETHER

All this work and you don't even have a course yet!? Sometimes it may feel that way, but putting all the planning and design time in up front will help to ensure the success of your project. Now it is time to start putting the course together.

During the production process, you'll want to keep a close eye on everything to make sure all the right criteria are met. This formative evaluation process ranges from simple proofreading, to content reviews, to functionality and technical testing, and finally to end-user testing.

You'll likely start off with a small manageable prototype and then revise and expand your guidelines as you prepare for full-scale production.

Rapid Prototyping

If you have a lot of courseware to develop and not a lot of time to do it, you may be tempted to jump right in and get everyone started. But if you are working on a course for the first time or are working on a course with significant design changes over previous courses, you might do well to start with a prototype.

A prototype is a sample chunk of courseware that is developed from start to finish before the rest of the courseware is begun. Rapid prototyping means developing a rather small, but representative chunk of content—perhaps five to 10 minutes' worth.

Why Create a Prototype?

During the design phase, you made a lot of assumptions and decisions. The prototype helps make sure that those assumptions are valid and that the decisions translate well when they move from the drawing board into actual production. Developing a prototype from beginning to end before starting work on the rest of the courseware has several benefits:

Saves Rework

During the prototype phase, you will probably find elements that don't work as intended or guidance that wasn't clear to writers, artists, or programmers. If you have already begun production on a number of lessons or modules, all of them will have to be revised once you learn of the issues. If you work with a prototype, you can catch the issues early and revise your design or processes before the rest of the work begins.

Helps Streamline Processes

During the development of the prototype, you will probably uncover various shortcuts that help the entire team work together. You may find that it is easier for your programmer to build the course if the storyboards use a certain style. Or you may learn from the person in charge of audio recording that if the script is provided in double-spaced format, there are fewer errors made during recording.

Helps With Development Estimates

By taking one chunk of content from beginning to end, you can test your development timelines and make revisions to the estimates. Realize, however, that the first part of any new course tends to take the longest.

Can Be Tested

If it turns out your courseware is too complicated for your target audience or the design style is too frivolous for the culture, then the prototype phase is the best place to find this out. Similarly, you can find out at this point if the course works technically in the target environment. This is accomplished with user testing and integration testing; both are covered in more detail later in this chapter. The sooner in the project you uncover an issue, the easier it is to resolve. If you wait until you are ready to launch a program, then you will have expensive, time-consuming revisions on your hands.

Helps You Feel the Progress

It can be good for team morale and customer comfort to see some very real, tangible progress on an e-learning project. The prototype is something you can show to everyone to build excitement, support, and momentum.

There is one major disadvantage to working with a prototype—time. Putting together a prototype can often take six to eight weeks because of all the decisions that have to be made, all the people who need to provide input, and all the processes that need to be worked out. This may feel like a very long time before you can really start the development. However, on most projects, it is worth the investment up front to save time, money, and headaches for the rest of the project.

 Tips From the Pros: Selecting the Content for a Prototype

When deciding what content to use for the prototype, think typical. You don't want to select the simplest material, and you don't want to select the most complex material. Instead, select something that is typical of the course in general and that incorporates the major features and functions of the course. For example, you probably don't want to select the beginning of the course since that material is often very general and may not lend itself to the interactions, practices, and quizzes you have planned for the rest of the course. Since prototypes tend to be more about design and functionality than about content, the screens you choose for the prototype don't have to be sequential.

Rapid Development

The process of developing an e-learning course from concept to execution can be a time-consuming endeavor. So if there is a need for immediate training, what can be done to minimize the gap between the time the course is needed and the time the course can comfortably be created? Is there a way to speed up the process?

Rapid development is the answer. It allows an e-learning course to be developed faster—and sometimes cheaper—without sacrificing quality. Here are some things that can decrease development time:

Developing Several Courses or Modules at the Same Time

Ideally, you would want to develop one course all the way to completion to serve as a prototype, and then begin the additional modules. If you need to save time, have your team start working on the storyboards for additional modules before you finish the prototype. If you use this strategy, plan on some rework being done on the storyboards based on lessons learned from the prototype—but at least you'll have a good start on your other modules' content.

Choosing an Easy-to-Learn Course Authoring Tool

If you have a tool that is easy to learn, you'll be up and running quickly, and you can probably find more people in your organization who can help you. Even the subject matter experts themselves can pitch in if it is easy enough to learn.

Choosing an Easy-to-Use Course Authoring Tool

Whether or not something is easy to learn is a one-time issue. Be sure also to consider how easy it is to use once you are up and running. The same module might take one hour in one software or three hours in another software.

Using Ready-Made Templates

When you use templates that are already created, you can just plug information into the template, rather than having to make individual interface design decisions. With the templates, the design has already been produced.

Wearing Lots of Hats

If there is someone on your development team who can design, develop, and program your e-learning course, let him or her do it! If the same person is writing the storyboards, working with the media elements, and assembling the course, you can save time for two reasons. First, the storyboard instructions don't have to be as detailed if one person is doing all the work. Secondly, any time work must pass from one person to another, a little time is lost and the project coordination effort increases. If one person is doing it all, you don't need that extra time.

Working on Media and Authoring Before the Review Cycle is Complete

Ideally, you would have your storyboards reviewed internally by your team as well as by your client (internal or external) and SMEs before you begin the process of finding or creating the graphics and actually assembling the course. However, the storyboard review cycles can take a lot of time and are prone to delays. If you need to accelerate your project, you can use the drafts of the storyboards to begin the work on the media and authoring. This will give you a head start on that work, but realize you may need to re-do some of it based on changes requested by the client or the SMEs.

Keeping on Top of Deadlines

The shorter the time allotted for course completion, the more crucial it is for you to make sure no deadlines are missed. Even one deadline being missed can be a problem when you are working toward rapid development.

The course authoring tool you choose is the most critical factor when you are working toward a rapid development goal. Look for one that contains good templates (or allows you to make your own) and is easy to use.

Paper Review Cycles

While you are still at the storyboard phase of development, changes are still relatively easy to fix. Therefore, it is usually a good idea to conduct a series of thorough reviews before the course is actually built. Once media has been developed and the course has been assembled, changes become more involved. However, if you need a quick turnaround, you can choose to hold off on all reviews until the course is built. In most cases, you will want to review storyboards for content, instructional design, and editorial accuracy.

Structuring Your Reviews

During the design phase, the process for handling storyboard and other reviews was defined and documented. There are many ways to structure your review cycles and many factors for you to consider, such as:

- How many people should look at a given module?
- When should external reviewers (business customers and subject matter experts) be involved? Should there be an internal review first? Should reviewers be involved at storyboard phase or once the course is developed?
- What if people disagree with each other in their comments?
- How long should reviewers be allowed to go over the material?
- What if they don't respond in the time allotted?
- How should feedback be provided? (for example, handwritten notes, Excel spreadsheet, tracked changes in Word)
- How will open issues and questions be tracked and handled?
- What if you think a suggested change isn't a good idea?
- How would extensive changes be handled? (Would the project schedule be affected? Should such changes be considered out of scope? If appropriate, would the requested changes warrant additional charges?)
- What is the process for checking that corrections were made properly?
- Should there be a formal sign-off on the final version?
- Can any media or programming work be done before final sign-off?

FIGURE 10-1: SAMPLE STORYBOARD REVIEW PROCESS

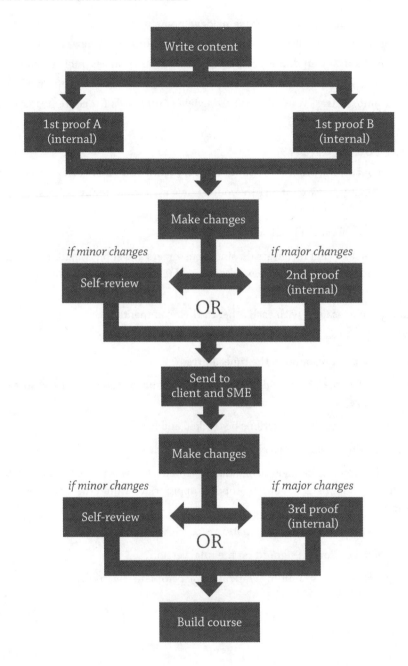

Content Review

You can have the flashiest graphics and the coolest interactions in the world, but if your content is inaccurate, your course will be a flop. That's why one of the early steps in the review process is to have your content checked for accuracy. Even if you are converting material from an existing document, you'll still want a thorough review—a simple edit could inadvertently change the meaning of something.

It's important to provide clear instructions to your reviewers; some might get caught up in grammar or typographical issues instead of focusing on the content itself. You increase the chances of getting the kind of feedback you want by providing elements you want reviewers to address.

Here are some content review questions you can ask:

- Are the objectives valid?
- Are the objectives complete? If someone masters all the stated objectives, will they have all the information they need to know?
- Is all of the information accurate, thorough, and current?
- Are there any terms or concepts used that the target audience may not already understand?
- Is there anything critical to mastering the objectives that has not been covered?
- Is there any information included in the course that the target audience doesn't really need to know?
- Are the explanations of the content clear and accurate?
- Are the diagrams, captions, and graphics accurate?
- Are all industry-specific terms spelled properly?
- If there is audio, are all industry-specific terms pronounced properly?
- Do the activities reinforce the most critical information?
- Do the questions test the most critical information?
- Would someone be prepared to do his or her job after completing this course?
- Has anything been left out?

Instructional Design Review

Once you have thorough, accurate content, you want to ensure it is being taught well. This is why you'll want your courses to be reviewed for instructional design. If you are a one-person team, then this step will be a self-check. Ideally, you would have a separate team member with knowledge of instructional design to review the work.

These steps should be on your instructional design review checklist:

- Review the Content Review Questions.

- Will the learners understand what is expected of them?

- Are the objectives well written and clearly stated?

- Are the benefits of learning this information clearly explained?

- Does the teaching content support the objectives?

- Will the learners know how to apply the information to their particular situation?

- Are the learners given opportunities to practice the concepts?

- Do the learners receive adequate feedback on their practice sessions?

- Are the questions too easy or too hard?

- Are any of the questions too subjective?

Editorial Review

In addition to the reviews of content and instructional design, you'll want to make sure your information is written, structured, and formatted correctly. This job can be filled by anyone with strong written language skills who has a copy of your standards documentation.

The editorial review and the instructional design review can be done by the same person, but preferably not at the same time. It's hard to wear both hats at once, so you'll get more thorough feedback if the reviewer goes through the material once for instructional design and then a second time for editorial issues.

Some teams prefer to save the editorial review until last, getting the big issues out of the way before starting on the smaller ones. That way you don't have to worry about grammar or word choice on a screen that is going to be rewritten by the subject matter experts anyway.

However, you may want to do an editorial review before sending storyboards to a client or subject matter experts so you don't risk being embarrassed by spelling and grammar problems or risk having them focus more on the typos than on the content issues you want them to address.

This is your editorial review checklist:

- Are there any spelling or typographical errors?

- Does the writing use good grammar and word choice?

- Could the same thing be said more simply? More concisely?

- Is the material written to the intended reading level?

- Are there any phrases or idioms that a nonnative speaker of English might not understand?

- Is the formatting consistent with the standards documentation and any designated style guide?

- For any formatting not specifically designated in the documentation, is it used consistently throughout the course?

Been There; Done That: Including Stakeholders Early in the Process

A large retailer created an e-learning course for some of its frontline employees. Just before the course was ready to go live, the team at headquarters who created the course gave a sneak preview to the regional managers. It turns out that the new course included a policy on a major customer service issue that many of the regional managers disagreed with. Before e-learning, headquarters created instructor-led materials, but the regional managers would just skip over any policies they didn't support. With a self-paced e-learning course, however, they did not have that freedom. They had no choice but to bring up their concerns about the policy—perhaps for the first time. The project had to be put on hold while the stakeholders discussed not just this one policy, but how much freedom regional managers should have on such issues.

Assembling the Course

The methods and processes you would use for assembling the course will vary greatly based on what kind of authoring tool you are using, as well as the specific course features and functions you are incorporating. At this stage in the project, you will be creating your media elements based on direction from the storyboards, and actually assembling all the content into whatever course-building system you are using.

You will be guided by all the decisions you made up until this point, specifically those found in your project plan, design document, and storyboards. Now it comes time to simply follow the directions. However, there are a few special concerns you might want to think about as well.

Course Extras

During production, it is easy to focus mainly on the individual modules or lessons. However, the development phase also includes any course extras that are a part of the design.

Based on your design plan, you may need to develop these additional course elements:

- title page: if you want a graphic or animated first impression for the course

- catalog description: to help the learners decide if a course is appropriate for them

- fine print: to provide any legal statements, such as copyright, confidentiality statement, privacy policy (especially if you will be tracking scores and answers), disclaimers, acknowledgements for other copyrighted material used with permission, and statements about trademarks referred to

- how to use this course: to provide details on the various features and functions of the course; for example, how to move around

- help section: to provide troubleshooting on issues that might arise with the course

- FAQs (Frequently Asked Questions): to give information either about how the course operates or about the content itself

- glossary and index

- references and job aids

- any other feature you might be including.

 Been There; Done That: Remember the Course Extras

You've got plenty of time to work on course extras, which is a blessing and a curse. Since they don't need to get done until the very end, they are often forgotten until the very end. Then there's a mad rush to get them finished in time—when they could have been developed and approved weeks or months earlier.

File Names and Version Control

Once production begins, you will be creating a lot of files: storyboard files, media elements, course files, and output files. Once you begin the review cycles, you are likely to have several versions of each. Special care needs to be taken to make sure that you know where to find everything and which version is the most current.

If you are using a learning content management system, you can manage files, versions, and reviews in the system itself. Otherwise, you will need to create standards and conventions to help. Here are a few suggestions:

- **Use separate folders to indicate where a given file is in the process**. For example, you can have a Storyboards folder with subfolders called "SB-rough draft," "SB-1st proof," "SB-ready for client review" and "SB-ready to program."

- **Use the file name to show where it is in the process**. For example, each reviewer can add his or her initials to the file name when finished reviewing it. "UnitA-de" could mean that it has been reviewed once and "UnitA-de-dw" could mean that is has been reviewed twice.

- **Keep a spreadsheet to track your progress and include a place to include file names and locations**. This will help you quickly locate the exact information you need later.

- **Use a standard file folder structure**. If you work on a team with several other people, anyone may need to step in and help out with a course. If everyone's files are structured differently, that may be difficult to do. Consider creating a standard folder structure to use for all projects.

FIGURE 10-2: SAMPLE FILE STRUCTURE

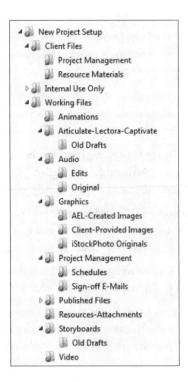

On-Screen Review Cycles

Even though your content was probably reviewed very thoroughly during the storyboard phase, you will want to have it reviewed again once it is built. During this phase, you'll want to revisit the questions you asked during the storyboard review (content, instructional design, and editorial reviews) to make sure that everything from the storyboards has been included in the online draft and that the concepts work as intended. In addition, you'll need to make sure everything functions properly and that the course meets the needs of the intended audience.

Content, Instructional Design, and Editorial Reviews

In addition to what you reviewed during the storyboard phase, a new part of the review at this point is a review of the media elements. You'll want to take a thorough look at graphics, interactions, audio, and video as you go through the three main review areas. Check for everything from typos in the graphics to proper pronunciation in the audio to changes needed to the instructions on an interaction because it was programmed differently than originally planned.

Functionality Review

FIGURE 10-3: SAMPLE ON-SCREEN REVIEW PROCESS

In addition to reviewing content, you'll want to make sure the course has been programmed properly and functions as expected. The best quality assurance (QA) tester is one who enjoys trying to "break" the system, gets the course to do something it shouldn't do, and looks at everything a learner might possibly misunderstand or do wrong.

The types of issues you should look for will vary based on the specific features and functions of your course, your development process, your authoring tool, and lessons learned from previous mistakes. For example, if your course-authoring process includes an automatic screen counter, you may not need to go through the whole course and make sure the number is right on each page (except perhaps for the prototype where you test to make sure the function is working). However, if you have to manually enter the page counter, then you would want to check it on every screen. You may want to create a checklist similar to Figure 10-4.

To help manage the review and revision process, create a checklist for the reviewers and a tracking log for requesting, making, and confirming corrections. A sample format is provided for your reference. You will need to add your own elements based on your unique situation. For example, Figure 10.5 includes a column for issue type. For large development teams with clearly defined roles, this is a useful column that lets team members find and fill in the issues that relate to them, such as audio, graphics, text, programming. If you are a one- or two-person team that does everything, then this column may not be necessary.

FIGURE 10-4: ON-SCREEN FUNCTIONALITY CHECKLIST

ISSUE TYPE	ISSUE	MODULE								
		A	B	C	D	E	F	G	H	I
Overall Module										
Navigation	Each section launches from menu									
Navigation	All screens are present									
Navigation	Screen counter is accurate									
Navigation	Forward through the course									
Navigation	Back through the course									
Navigation	Module title is accurate									
Per Screen (all screen types)										
Programming	Slide heading correct									
Programming	Text taken from the correct storyboard									
Programming	No text cut off									
Text formatting	Text formatted properly (bullets, bolding)									
Text	Text clear, true, and error free									
Media	Correct media shown									
Buttons	Unneeded buttons are inactive									
Rollover or Pop-up Screens										
Rollover	Rollover text matches image									
Rollover	Text does not overlap									
Rollover	Clear what has been accessed or not									
Text	Easy to understand what to do									
Buttons	Forward button does not work until complete									
Computer Simulation Screens										
Buttons	Show Me button launches simulation									
Media	Simulation plays to the end									
Buttons	Pause works									
Buttons	Replay works									
Buttons	Forward button does not work until complete									
Practice Screens										
Programming	Get all answers right									
Programming	Get all answers wrong									
Programming	First incorrect feedback									
Programming	Second incorrect feedback									
Programming	Try to do something you shouldn't be able to									
Buttons	Show Me button inactive									
Buttons	Forward button does not work until complete									

FIGURE 10-5: SAMPLE ON-SCREEN ISSUES LIST

Slide	Issue Details	Type	Updates	Status	Discuss Client	Discuss Internal	Client Action	Audio Re-record
28	10 Make updates to the email that were made on slide 4	text		made				
29	4 Outlook interface, crop out the toolbars and start with the send, from, to section	image	DE: De made the original graphic (D - Need the original pieces to make this edit)	made		Y		
30	5 Re-work this image. Space out the levels so that you can make the arrows more prominent. Animate arrows to show the flow of information. (up in first paragraph and down on the second paragraph)	image	DE: Jim made the original graphic. (D - Recreated image using Storyline objects)	made				
31	5 Delete last sentence in audio, and make audio edit in storyboards	audio		made				Y
32	6 Come up with a new graphic -- they don't like the spoke concept	image	D - Went with a tin can phone concept since this is about communication.	made				
33	6 Make the pop-ups required...add "visited" indicators	logic	D - Initial State of the Next button is Disabled until all the States of the four callouts have changed to Visited.	made				
34	6 Add instructions in audio	audio	D - I did not see the audio for the instructions in the Edits folder.	issue		Y		Y
35	7 They'll provide a new image.	image		made				

Plan on how you would like to handle a review of the reviews. It is dangerous to assume that all problems got fixed properly without creating any new problems. It is more time consuming but generally worthwhile to have someone confirm every correction, including every correction to a correction.

Technical Testing

While the course may work properly for the designers, developers, and testers, you'll also want to make sure it functions properly on the target platform. Generally, this testing will be conducted or at least coordinated with your IT department. These are some testing types:

Integration Testing

Do the courses operate properly with any other related systems (such as a learning management system)?

Load Testing

Will the courses, when used by the projected number of people, cause the systems to slow down or even crash? Can the servers handle it? Can the company bandwidth handle it?

Workstation Testing

Will the courses run on the various configurations of workstations? You'll want to test the courses on the various configurations possible, such as different devices, browser versions, operating systems, or bandwidth. If you are dealing with learners taking the course from their home computers, be sure to test for all the variations that might exist on a home computer. If learners will be dialing in through a network (such as Citrix), consider any restrictions or special configurations for that network.

Technical testing is an area where your prototype will be extremely valuable. It is quite possible that you'll find issues that affect some significant aspect of your design. Make sure you get that feedback early in the development process.

 Been There; Done That: Remote Access

A Fortune 500 company was rolling out a course to train employees on a new computer system. The course was tested and worked perfectly from the workstations in the office. Just before the course went live, someone tested it from home using the company's secure remote access system. When viewing the course through this system, the course played in the remote access system's browser, not the browser on the learner's computer. It turns out, the remote access system was using an old browser version that caused problems with the course. The course had to go on hold for a full month until the browser version could be updated in the remote access system.

End-User Testing

If you conduct testing with subject matter experts, instructional designers, editors, and technical testers, you will greatly improve the quality of the course. But despite all of that hard work, that doesn't mean your ultimate learners will like it, enjoy it, be able to use it, or get what they need from it. That's why you may want to include end-user testing, also known as pilot testing.

User testing will help you determine whether:

- they like or enjoy the course
- they understand the material
- the material is helpful to them
- they know and can do what they need to as a result of the course
- they can operate the course.

According to Margaret Driscoll and Saul Carliner (2005) in *Advanced Web-Based Training Strategies: Unlocking Instructionally Sound Online Learning*, "a study compared the number of problems found in a draft by usability experts with those actually encountered by users. The 'best' expert could only find 48 percent of the roadblocks that users found (Boren and Ramey 2000). This means that the only way to effectively identify roadblocks is through a usability test."

Planning Your User Testing

You'll want your test subjects to represent the full cross section of your audience—include computer proficiency, age, cultural background, existing knowledge of the subject matter, role in the company, and any other variable that relates to your program.

Make sure that the learners will have everything they need to complete the course. This includes a proper technical setup (such as the proper plug-ins or speakers), as well as any supplemental materials required for the course (a printed manual or paper and pencil). You may also need to set up user names and passwords for each tester.

Check with your facilitator to coordinate the length of the test, the number of learners that can be observed by a single facilitator, and any supplies needed (such as forms and pencils).

 The Great Debate: Timing of User Testing

When do you conduct user testing? It's great to get feedback early, but most end users aren't likely to sit down and read storyboards. And you may not want to show them the first draft of your online course because it still has things you want to change. So it might be best to wait until the end to show it to them. However, if you wait until the end, any change they suggest will take that much longer to fix because everything has been built, reviewed, fixed, and approved.

Conducting Your User Testing

Whenever possible, you'll want someone who has not been involved with the development to conduct the testing. The users are likely to be more comfortable sharing feedback, and the facilitators are more likely to remain neutral about the process and the feedback.

Additionally, it is best to work with someone who has experience with user testing and knows the best way to gather complete, accurate, detailed feedback. You can't expect your test subjects to tell you everything you need to know by filling out a quick form. You'll want to work with a facilitator who is skilled at getting strong feedback.

Ideally, the facilitator will gather feedback by observing the learners taking the course, by encouraging the learners to make verbal comments about their thoughts while they are taking the course, and by conducting a final interview to get more details and clarify comments.

If in-person testing with a facilitator is not feasible, you can also use third-party services to record the screens of the users as they take your course.

Acting on Your Results

Imagine you are reviewing the summary of the results, and you see that about a third of the test subjects say the course was too slow. Another third say it was too fast. And another third say it was just right. It's enough to make you feel like Goldilocks and go take a nap!

Review and consider all comments, but then make your best judgment. You'll have comments that contradict each other. Some suggestions would be too expensive or time consuming to implement, some would result in a worse product, and some comments might even come across as rude or insensitive.

You'll have to strike a delicate balance between deciding that a comment is not valid or universal enough to warrant a change versus disregarding a comment because deep down you resent it.

 Tips From the Pros: Interpreting Feedback

Unfortunately, you'll not always get clear feedback from your test subjects. Sometimes they'll comment on what they think the solution is, rather than what the problem is. Sometimes they'll be too vague to really give you an idea of what could be different.

For example, if a learner says the course is too long, is it really too long? Maybe it only felt long because the learner wasn't interested and couldn't figure out how it applied to him or her. In this case, deciding to shorten the course wouldn't fix the real problem.

Try, whenever possible, to elicit more information from the tester, or at least get more creative when reviewing a comment and try to ensure you're really getting to the heart of the issue.

Be sure to build time and money into your project plan for the rework that will come from your testing. It's nice to think that everything will work out as planned, but experience tends to prove otherwise.

Summary

It's exciting to see your course finally taking shape and coming to life. By starting with a prototype, not only will you have the chance to build excitement by seeing some tangible results quickly, but you'll also gain valuable insight about your design and development that will streamline your production and increase your course's effectiveness.

In addition to the actual production work itself, take the time necessary to build in all the checks and balances needed to ensure that you finish with a superior product that works properly, people enjoy, and that meets the business goal.

Remember to put formal processes in place to review your course for content, instructional design, editorial issues, proper functionality, technical problems, and end-user feedback.

11

THE IMPLEMENTATION PHASE

So, your courses are finished. You've put your time and energy into making everything perfect. You can finally breathe easy because your work is done. Now you just get to sit back and relax and let everybody take your courses . . . or can you? Almost, but not quite.

Have you ensured that everything and everyone is ready for the courses? For example, do the learners know why they are taking them? Do they know how to access them? Will they get the needed support from management to find the time for the courses? What will happen once they complete a course?

Implementation day is when the courses are available for your first learner. But prior to that day, it's important to consider and execute some key details to ensure successful implementation.

Preparing the Audience

If you build it, will they come? You'll increase your chances if they know where to go, why it is important to them, and if they have the support of management to do so. You'll want to market your course to the organization so people will get excited and know what to do.

Your preparation approach might be different based on where your course falls in the e-learning rollout. If the course is the first e-learning course ever, you may want to take more time and care to prepare your audience than if e-learning has already been embraced by your organization as a regular training method.

Managers and Supervisors

Getting buy-in from the management team is often the best way for training to be disbursed through an organization. The management team (hopefully) wants what is best for the organization, for themselves, and for the people working for them. They have great influence over the audience members, who may or may not be ready and able to participate in training.

Often the best way to get buy-in from management is to give business reasons for the training. For example, in a customer-service organization, a particular course may likely lead to more satisfied customers, which could ultimately make their lives easier. Letting the managers know about this benefit could give them the incentive to encourage the learners.

The best time to get buy-in from managers and supervisors is early in the project. For smaller projects, you will probably do this during project initiation. For projects that might be rolled out to hundreds or thousands of employees, it won't be feasible to include all the managers and supervisors early in the process. Have a plan in place to reach them at the most appropriate (and feasible) time.

Learners

It can be challenging to inform learners about the course and the learning process. Marketing the course through email, company literature, and an Internet or intranet site are all possible options, and don't forget to use your management team.

The management team can introduce the training and create urgency for course completion. Giving information on how learning the course information could help learners or how it could make their jobs easier might be good self-motivation. In some cases, if it's important to an organization, making a course mandatory might be a step toward ensuring its completion.

Environment

Has e-learning been launched before in the organization? And, how do the learners feel about e-learning? How do they feel about training in general?

The learning environment can make or break an e-learning project. If e-learning is new, you may want to take extra time marketing the concept and the process, as well as the course. Perhaps you can offer a classroom session for everyone to try out the first course. This helps bridge the gap for learners between how they are accustomed to learning and how they will soon be learning.

If e-learning has been rolled out and was unsuccessful in the past, you'll want to fix what went wrong during the first rollout, market the course as "new," and focus on course improvements and benefits. Consider asking a core group of influential employees (not necessarily managers, but peers who are well respected) to serve as a pilot group. If they like the new training, they'll spread the word, and people will listen.

If your organization has rolled out e-learning successfully and the environment is positive, you may only need to mention a course exists and everybody will want to take it.

Incentives and Disincentives

Incentives are anything that encourage a learner to take a course or series of courses. An incentive could be as simple as a certificate of completion or a type of bonus. Incentives can give e-learning a positive reputation in the company as they encourage participation and excitement.

Disincentives, however, are anything that may discourage someone from taking a course. Sometimes courses have unintentional, built-in disincentives. For example, it is a disincentive if learners must spend an hour taking a course, yet they still have to achieve the same production levels as if they were on the manufacturing floor all day. It is a disincentive if there are consequences to not completing work, but no consequences for not completing training.

Take a look at everything from manager attitudes to performance criteria to bonus policies to see where you can add incentives and remove disincentives.

Hoo-Hah

What is *hoo-hah*? Some very technical e-learning terminology? No, it's just a catch-all word for anything fun and interesting you might want to do to get people excited. Especially if an e-learning initiative is a new concept, the hoo-hah can help the course get the attention it needs to be successful.

Hoo-hah might include creating a fun name for the overall initiative with its own logo. You could put up signs, posters, or balloons. You might have drawings or other contests for the first people to complete a course. You could have a kick-off party with the CEO or other high-profile executives (and lots of food!).

Take some time to think about the best ways to include a little fanfare with your rollout. Every organization has a culture or personality, and your company culture will dictate how much and what type of hoo-hah is best.

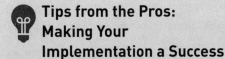

**Tips from the Pros:
Making Your
Implementation a Success**

1. Develop an engaging e-learning course. (If the course is bad, no amount of marketing will lead to long-term success.)
2. Make your course match your audience's learning needs.
3. Market your e-learning course.
4. Provide support. (Your support needs will be greatest in the first few months but then should dwindle some.)
5. Give clear directions on how to access the course.
6. Give incentives for course completion.
7. Minimize disincentives.
8. Involve management to promote buy-in.
9. Support a positive environment for e-learning.
10. Prepare your technology for your course so your first learners have a positive experience and spread the word.

Ongoing Management

Once your course is up and running, you'll want to continue to manage it, looking out for any technical problems, as well as providing necessary updates and revisions.

Troubleshooting

No matter how much time you spent reviewing and testing your course, there will probably be some type of technical problems. Perhaps it is a home user with a different browser or the realization that the courses won't run on your remote network. While you can't prevent all of these issues, you can be prepared for them. Make sure you have sufficient project resources (time, staff, and money) to troubleshoot issues as they arise.

Revisions and Updates

As a course ages, it may need to be revised or updated. Revisions could be done simply to make the course better based on feedback received, or updates may be needed for information that has changed and is no longer valid. Sometimes, the problem is that nobody planned on revising or updating the course, so it isn't being managed.

Have a plan in place to deal with policy changes, computer upgrades, or learner feedback. Decide in advance who will be the long-term "owner" of the training program. In some organizations, it is a different group than the one that created the courses initially.

Reporting

You can set your course up to give feeds to your LMS to track any number of things—but if you don't check what it's tracking, it doesn't help you evaluate your course. You may want to evaluate test questions, for example, to make sure they are reliable and valid or check your pass/fail rate or completion rate. Chapter 12 provides more information on what to consider in the evaluation phase.

Summary

Once your courses are complete, it takes more to implement them than just posting them on the servers. After making sure your courses function properly, your technology is set, and your audience is informed and excited, you can invite your audience to start learning.

Remember, however, that training development is never truly over. Put plans in place to troubleshoot issues, update content, and manage the administrative elements.

So, now you can finally breathe easy because your work is done. Sit back and relax and let everybody take your course . . . until it's time for the next one.

12

THE EVALUATION PHASE

You did it! You have e-learning content up and running! Is it everything you hoped for? And is it everything that everyone else hoped for?

You have used a number of evaluation techniques to guide you during the development of the project (formative evaluation). Now it is time to evaluate the reaction, effectiveness, and impact of the final product (summative evaluation).

One of the most commonly used models for evaluating training is the Kirkpatrick model, developed by Donald Kirkpatrick:

- Level 1: Reaction
- Level 2: Learning
- Level 3: Behavior
- Level 4: Results

Many training practitioners work with an additional, fifth, level, as suggested by ROI expert Jack Phillips—Level 5: Return on Investment

These forms of evaluation apply to any type of training: instructor led or e-learning. This chapter offers some guidelines about each level of evaluation plus specific information about what is unique to e-learning.

Level 1 Evaluation: Learner Reaction

Level 1 evaluation is designed for you to receive feedback about what the learners thought about the course.

Goal of Level 1 Evaluation

Find out the learners' opinions; for example, on whether they liked the course, whether they thought it was effective, or whether they thought they would use the information. A Level 1 evaluation is, by nature, very subjective—measuring opinions and impressions.

A positive reaction from the learners can affect whether or not they truly learned the information, as well as whether or not they are willing and eager to move forward with other, similar courses. However, it is not the same as whether or not they truly learned. (That's Level 2.)

As with the results of your pilot testing (chapter 10), you'll gather some information that is helpful, some that is vague, and some that is downright confusing.

Sample Questions for Evaluating Any Training Format

Consider using Likert Scale questions such as these, which learners would rate from 1 to 5 (agree to disagree, or similar):

- The course met my expectations.
- The course met my needs.
- I have information I can use on the job.
- The course was interesting.
- The course was enjoyable.
- The material was covered at just the right pace.
- The material was covered in the right depth.
- I would recommend this course to someone else.
- There was adequate opportunity for me to practice what I learned.

Short-answer questions such as these could be included:

- The most valuable thing I learned was:
- One way to make the course better would be to:

Questions Unique to an E-Learning Course

In addition to the information you've already gathered, you may also want to ask questions about the delivery method, the technology, and the ease of use, with Likert Scale questions such as these:

- The course was easy to use.

- The course had no technical problems.

- The course downloaded quickly.

You could include a short-answer question:

- How would you describe your experience with the online format of this course?

Based on your particular programs, you may also want to ask other questions; for example, to assess the registration process and the discussion forums.

Methods for Collecting Data

You might design a Level 1 evaluation for an e-learning course to appear automatically in the course at the end, to launch automatically when the user exits, or to be emailed to the user after the fact. It may be created and managed through your authoring tool, through your learning management system, or just through your email system.

The challenge with a Level 1 evaluation in the e-learning world is persuading your learners to complete the survey. There is no instructor standing at the door asking them for the evaluation before they leave. Therefore, you may want to consider various follow-up methods or motivation strategies to encourage completion of the survey. For example:

- Make sure the survey pops up for the user, rather than just providing a link they must click.

- Send reminder emails to anyone who hasn't completed a survey.

- Require an evaluation to be filled out before a certificate can be issued.

- Enter each person who completes the survey into a drawing for a prize.

Level 2 Evaluation: Learning

With a Level 2 evaluation, you are trying to determine if the learners actually learned what they were supposed to learn. Did they meet the objectives?

Testing Within the Course

In most cases, the Level 2 evaluation is done with some sort of post-test that is part of the course. Testing was covered in detail in chapter 7. You may choose to have only a post-test to determine the learners' ending level of knowledge. Or, if appropriate, you may include a pre-test and a post-test so you can see the difference and assess how much of their final knowledge is a result of the course itself.

Blended Approaches

Based on the course's objectives and the type of content, some of the Level 2 evaluation may be conducted in person. You may need the learner to demonstrate a specific skill, speak about an attitude, or demonstrate a behavior in a real-world environment. In these situations, you may have an instructor or mentor moderate an assessment in order to determine the learner's mastery of the objectives. For example, a medical technician course may teach the proper procedures and techniques for drawing blood. But when it comes time for the learner to graduate, he or she needs to perform the procedure on a medical dummy with feedback from an instructor.

Validating Your Tests

In order for you to be able to trust the results of your Level 2 testing, your questions need to be well designed. During the design and development of the course, make sure the questions adequately test the objectives, aren't too easy or too hard, are legally sound, and are fairly safeguarded against cheating.

Once the tests have been developed and deployed, you may want to review overall scores per question. This can help identify possible problems with either the question or the content. If you find that most questions, on average, have about an 85 percent success rate, but there is one question with a 35 percent success rate, you might have an issue. You can then review the question and the related content to try to rectify the situation. There are several possible causes:

- The question was programmed incorrectly.
- The directions are unclear.
- The question is unclear.
- The question is misleading.
- The answers are too subjective.
- The related content was not covered adequately in the course (not covered at all, not covered in sufficient detail, not explained clearly, or not given enough emphasis).

Levels 3–5 Evaluation: Impact

In a corporate environment, you generally don't train just to train. You generally don't spend the time and effort to develop and deliver a course just for the sake of having the knowledge. You want to accomplish something. You want people to do something differently. You have a business goal, a change you want to see. That's why you learned about establishing the business goals of the course in chapter 2. Evaluation Levels 3, 4, and 5 help you determine the impact of the training.

Level 3: Behavior

A Level 3 evaluation helps you to determine whether or not learners' behaviors actually changed as a result of new learning. For example, you'll want to find out if they are doing what they are supposed to be doing (or not doing what they are not supposed to be doing).

A Level 3 evaluation is generally conducted three to six months after the training and is often done in the actual work environment. Some methods to find out if the skills, knowledge, or attitudes are being put into practice on the job by the learners include observations and surveys with supervisors, customers, or co-workers.

These are some examples of observation checklist items or survey questions:

- Does the subject use protective eyewear when operating the machinery?
- Does the subject verify the identity of the customer before answering questions about an account?
- Does the subject ask for additional leads from the customer?

Level 4: Results

Before you embarked on your training initiative, someone in the organization believed that training would benefit the organization in some way. A Level 4 evaluation proves (or disproves) that belief. The learners may have enjoyed the class, learned what they were supposed to learn, and even used the information properly on the job. Those things alone, however, do not mean the business results were automatically achieved. For example, did safety incidents really go down? Did sales really go up?

The challenge with a Level 4 evaluation is that there are often many factors involved in a business issue. Even if the training is effective, another factor may have prevented the issue being resolved or improved. Conversely, the training may have been ineffective, while another factor was successful in resolving the issue. How do you know if training can take any of the credit or blame?

Unfortunately, there is no good answer to that question. You can, at least, do your best to measure the improvements desired. Refer to your business case to see what you hoped to accomplish, such as increased sales, reduced complaints, reduced turnover, increased efficiency, increased production, and fewer accidents. Then you can gather data on these outcomes. You'll probably want to identify other factors that also may have affected the results.

Level 5: Return on Investment (ROI)

Some training practitioners consider ROI to be a part of Level 4, while others consider it as its own level. Regardless of what level you put it in, you may want to attach dollar figures to your business results. Just as you looked at the potential ROI when you were deciding to embark on this endeavor (chapter 2), you can use the same guidelines to calculate the actual ROI.

Summary

An e-learning project is a significant endeavor. A lot of time, money, and effort probably went into it, so it makes sense to stop and see if it was worth it. Unfortunately, many companies do not take these steps because evaluation, too, takes time, money, and effort. The best way to ensure that you are able to undertake an evaluation effort is to build it into your project plan from the very beginning.

13

MOVING FORWARD

This book has walked you through the steps for taking your e-learning course from an idea to full-scale implementation. You have learned the process of conducting your needs analysis, designing your course, developing the different elements that will meet your objectives, implementing what you have created, and then evaluating your course.

You've learned about the many facets of e-learning planning, design, and development. You may decide to specialize in certain areas, or you may become a one-person team capable of creating courses from start to finish.

The future of e-learning continues to change as technology advances, as new ideas are implemented and tested, and as more and more companies implement e-learning initiatives. You'll want to stay on top of the changes so you can grow with them.

Here are some tips to help you move forward.

Find Your Path

You learned in chapter 3 that there are many specialized talents and roles you may need for your e-learning course:

- instructional designer
- researcher
- writer

- proofreader
- editor
- programmer for course assembly
- graphic designer
- quality assurance tester
- project manager
- subject matter expert
- voice talent
- audio recording and editing specialist
- video production and editing specialist.

As you decide where you fit in the e-learning landscape, ask yourself:

- Which of these interest me?
- Which of these am I already good at?
- Which of these would I like to learn more about?
- Which of these are in high demand in my area?

Keep Learning

There are formal and informal methods, free and paid, to help you become better at e-learning management, design, and development. There is a rich network of resources available to you to help build new skills and keep your existing skills current. For further information, refer to the annotated list of additional resources on this book's companion website: www.td.org/elearningtools.

Summary

During the past few years, the e-learning field has grown exponentially. With this growth comes a need for e-learning professionals to stay current with the e-learning technology, hone current skills, and add new ones. As you prepare for the future, keep your sights on what is possible for you as an e-learning professional.

REFERENCES

Allen, M., and R. Sites. 2012. *Leaving ADDIE for SAM: An Agile Model for Developing the Best Learning Experiences.* Alexandria, VA: ASTD Press.

ATD Research. 2014. *Playing to Win: Gamification and Serious Games in Organizational Learning.* Alexandria, VA: ASTD Press.

Bean, C. 2014. *The Accidental Instructional Designer: Learning Design for the Digital Age.* Alexandria, VA: ASTD Press.

Bingham, T., and M. Conner. 2010. *The New Social Learning: A Guide to Transforming Organizations Through Social Media.* Alexandria, VA: ASTD Press.

Boren, M.T., and J. Ramey. 2000. "Thinking Aloud: Reconciling Theory and Practice." *IEEE Transactions on Professional Communication*, volume 43, number 3, 261–278.

Bozarth, J. 2010. *Social Media for Trainers: Techniques for Enhancing and Extending Learning.* San Francisco: Pfeiffer.

Carliner, S. 2003. *Training Design Basics.* Alexandria, VA: ASTD Press.

Driscoll, M., and S. Carliner. 2005. *Advanced Web-Based Training Strategies: Unlocking Instructionally Sound Online Learning.* San Francisco: Pfeiffer.

Halls, J. 2012. *Rapid Video Development for Trainers.* Alexandria, VA: ASTD Press.

Hodell, C. 2006. *ISD From the Ground Up.* Alexandria, VA: ASTD Press.

References

Kapp, K. 2012. *The Gamification of Learning and Instruction: Game-Based Methods and Strategies for Training and Education*. Alexandria, VA: ASTD Press.

Kapp, K., and R.A. Defelice. 2009. "Time to Develop One Hour of Training." ATD Learning Circuits Blog, August 31.www.td.org/Publications/Newsletters/Learning-Circuits/Learning-Circuits-Archives/2009/08/Time-to-Develop-One-Hour-of-Training.

Lewis, J.P. 2006. *The Fundamentals of Project Management*. 3rd ed. New York: AMACOM.

Mager, R. 1997. *Measuring Instructional Results (The Mager Six-Pack)*. 3rd ed. Atlanta: CEP.

Piskurich, G. 2006. *Rapid Instructional Design: Learning ID Fast and Right*. San Francisco: Pfeiffer.

"Section 508.gov: Opening Doors to IT." www.section508.gov.

Stolovitch, H.D., and E.J. Keeps. 2011. *Telling Ain't Training*. 2nd ed. Alexandria, VA: ASTD Press.

"United States Access Board: Advancing Full Access and Inclusion for All." www.access-board.gov.

United States Department of Defense. 1999. *Department of Defense Handbook: Development of Interactive Multimedia Instruction (IMI)*. Department of Defense. www.au.af.mil/au/awc/awcgate/dod/hbk3.pdf.

ABOUT THE AUTHORS

Diane Elkins and **Desirée Pinder** are the co-founders of Artisan E-Learning, a custom e-learning development company specializing in Articulate Studio, Storyline, Captivate, and Lectora. Throughout their 11 years in business, they have helped companies and individuals get started in e-learning. They are co-authors of the popular *E-Learning Uncovered* book series and speak regularly at national conferences such as ATD's International Conference & Exposition and TechKnowledge, E-Learning Guild Learning Solutions and DevLearn, and the Lectora User's Conference. They both have served on the board of their local ATD chapters.